Shannon & Jamie!

Many blessings on

your book births!

Julie

Somewhere Between
Double Trouble and Infinity

Julie Grace Strong-Chai

Somewhere Between
Double Trouble and Infinity

©

Julie Grace Strong-Chai

United States Copyright, 1999
Sunstar Publishing, Ltd.
204 South 20th Street
Fairfield, Iowa 52556

Library of Congress Catalog Card Number: 97-061875

ISBN 1-887472-42-8

Cover Design: Janean Strong
Amanda Collett

Readers interested in obtaining further information on the.subject matter of
this book are invited to correspond with The Secretary, Sunstar Publishing, Ltd.
204 South 20th Street, Fairfield, Iowa 52556

Dedication

❦ *I would like to dedicate this book to my parents, whose nurture, guidance, support and love have made it all possible.*

Sometimes the deepest, most intimate part of our life goes untold and those we love have only an inkling of the stories of our souls reflected in the mirror of our lives. Why this is true I do not know.

By example, my parents have taught me about unconditional love and grace. And although lessons like keeping my room clean and not belching in public did not always hold, the ones of eternal importance did and for that, I am grateful. My story may be a bit outside of the norm, yet I like to think that they are honored to know that the daughter they told to "just be yourself" is learning to be exactly that.

In Appreciation

A note of thanks to all who have encouraged me to write about my soul path and to those who have supported me along the way. To my parents and my husband without whose love and financial support this work would not have been possible. To my sister for her love, encouragement and creative partnership. To my dogs Noon-sup and Girl who teach me to notice the moment and not forget to play.

Thanks to Richard Fuller whose generous, cheerful and love-filled encouragement has been deeply appreciated. Thanks to Rodney Charles who had the courage and conviction to begin a small publishing company in rural Iowa and welcome the works of unknown writers like myself. A special thanks to Isabelle Hubert, my editor, whose immediate connection to the spirit of this book brought tears to my eyes and who, by grace, has helped me to "describe the silence". And finally, thanks to my clients who have allowed me the honor of helping them walk their own soul path and witness the splendor of the soul unfold.

Namaste.

Table Of Contents

Part Two — Savoring

Part Three—Responding
Chapter 11 — Lessons in Mindfulness

Chapter 12 — Responding with Others

Chapter 13 — Moving Out into the World

Part Four — Random Reflections on the Soul Path

All things are resolved
and there is from the clatter of thoughts
a silence
and from the shaking of emotions
a calm.
If I were to write what today is my thought
tomorrow it would not be
for it would blend into the silence
and become me.

Preface

> 🌿 *We all have a soul path that calls out to us.*
>
> *It is our connection with the Source and stirs underneath our anxiety, our discontent as well as our bliss. It is the real story of who we are that lies beneath who we were taught we should be. May my attempts to walk my soul path offer promise to those of you seeking to walk your own.*

Having entered into the deep mystery of the soul with my clients and honoring the sacredness of their human/divine journey, I am ready to honor my own by publicly giving it voice. All of it. The divine and the foolish, the joy and the pain.

> 🌿 *For me, the inner message and life has to be consistent with the outer message and life. I like that. I call it integrity.*

I hope that being honest about my journey and claiming the lessons and gifts which I have been able to discern, will help the reader to discover, explore and share their own.

May the Mystery We Call God bless the writing and the reading of these words. And may your own journey be blessed with love.

Finally, let me say that though my journey is filled with what might be called mystical experiences, these are by no means a sign of enlightenment. They just are and I offer them as that. I have much to learn and lots of room for growth. I would not trust anyone who claims that they don't.

> *Mystical experiences are simply doors opening into the spiritual realm.*
> *For me, they have offered proof of spirit and taught me things I might not have learned any other way.*
> *They are gifts which are awesome and humbling.*
> *They are not intended to be fuel for the ego.*

On that note, I close with these words from the apostle Paul which are as fitting for us today as they were for the group in Corinth two thousand years ago:

If I speak in the tongues of angels but do not have love, I am a noisy gong or a clanging cymbal.

And if I have prophetic powers, and understand all mysteries and all knowledge, and if I have faith, so as to move mountains, but do not have love, I am nothing.

If I give away all my possessions, and if I hand over my body so that I may boast, but do not have love, I gain nothing.

Love is patient; love is kind; love is not envious or boastful. It is not arrogant or rude.

Love does not insist on its own way; it is not irritable or resentful; it does not rejoice in wrongdoing but rejoices in the truth.

Love bears all things, believes all things, hopes all things and endures all things.

Love never ends.

— Corinthians 13:1-8

Part One

Noticing

Inside each of us
there awaits
a wonder
full
spirit of freedom

she waits
to dance
in the rooms
of our hearts
that are closed
dark and cluttered

she waits
to dance
in the spaces
where negative feelings
have built barricades
and stock-piled weapons

she waits
to dance
in the corners
where we still
do not believe
in our goodness

inside each of us
there awaits
a wonder
full
spirit of freedom

she will lift light feet
and make glad songs
within us
on the day
we open the door of ego
and let the enemies
stomp out

Excerpt from "The Star In My Heart: Experiencing Sophia, Inner Wisdom",
Joyce Rupp, 1990. Reprinted by permission of Innisfree Press, Philadelphia, PA.

Chapter 1

TIME TO REMEMBER

I loved the long trail rides on my horse in the Minnesota woods. I remember one day when my horse and I were leaving a field to enter the woods. It was just at the transitional point between field and woods and I was transfixed by the surroundings. The smell of fallen leaves and the sight of the trees changing color. The sound of a small stream rippling past the rocky soil. The feel of a gently caressing breeze.

> *There was a time*
> *when life for me was less cluttered.*
> *When things did not muffle the voice of God*
> *or block my vision of the miraculous.*
> *It was a time of great freedom,*
> *encompassing both joy and sorrow.*
> *A time of spiritual presence,*
> *mystical insight*
> *and visions.*
> *I knew that I was not really alone*
> *and the line between now and eternity*
> *was faded.*

We stopped. Horse and rider, one. I knew that this moment was holy and we were on sacred ground. I was aware that I had caught my breath, as if holding it would make the moment last. Then a wiser inner voice informed me that only by releasing my breath could I breathe again and that this experience was not one to capture but rather one to experience as a flow. Indeed, by trying to capture it, I lost it. By breathing, receiving in and releasing out, I continued to enjoy it.

Another memorable trail ride took place down a gravel country road. My horse was just walking along and we were taking in the scenery, in no hurry to be anywhere else. On the left side of the road, behind a wire fence, a herd of dairy cows were feeding in the field. One cow took notice of us and came to the fence. My horse took notice of the cow and walking over to the fence, stretched out his long neck to meet his new friend nose to nose.

For the longest time they simply stood still, exchanging breath while I framed the picture in my heart. I'm not sure what took place between them but it felt as if there was a common spirit that they shared, something that bound them, bound us together. Then, just as their greeting ended, I reached down and touched the hard, slippery wet nose of our sister the cow.

I was deeply moved and reflected upon our encounter as my horse and I continued down the road. Suddenly an inner voice broke through my thoughts asking, "If you like cows so much, why do you kill them?" Indignant, I replied "But I don't!" "Oh yes you do!" came the response. "You kill them when you eat them." I had never realized that before. I reflected upon this for the rest of the ride. Within the year, I became a vegetarian, but agreed to eat fish, at my mother's request.

One of our favorite rides took us past an apple tree in a small overgrown meadow not too far from the side of the road. My horse and I would stop to feast on a few tart, crispy apples so freely given by the tree. Sometimes I would get down and offer him the apple on foot. Then I could kiss his soft muzzle and bask in his warm fresh apple breath.

 With no obligations and no
demands upon us,
my horse and I explored forests, fields and
quiet meadows.
We greeted each life we encountered and
relished the beauty and mystery of it all.
I thought it would always be this way.

Chapter 2

DEATH OPENS MY EYES TO THE SPIRIT

First Conscious Encounter With the Spiritual/Mystical Realm

It started in a strange and subtle way that only made sense two weeks later. My first boyfriend, Philippe, and I had just come back from our last date before I was to leave Switzerland for college in New York. I vividly recall our last conversation as we sat outside my parents home in his VW.

"Why are you wearing that religious medallion around your neck?"I asked.

"It is a St. Christopher medal. It will protect me in the car."

The thought, "No, it won't," flashed through my mind. I had no idea where it came from. I left the car with a feeling of distance between us, as though I would never see him again. It didn't make sense since we were planning to get together at Christmas.

Two weeks into my upstate New York college adventure I suddenly began crying. I couldn't tell anyone why I was crying because I didn't know myself. So when people asked me what was wrong, all I could say was, "I don't know but I am going back to Switzerland."

That evening, at a student meeting with the dean, the dean came over to me and asked if I had a friend named Philippe back in Switzerland. I said yes. She said, "I'm very sorry to have to inform you that ...your friend died in a car accident."

Shock and grief had pretty much overwhelmed me, so I don't remember many details. I caught a flight back to Switzerland the next day, arriving in time for his funeral in a Catholic Church. It was the first funeral I had ever attended. Only one event stands out with great clarity. I was standing between his parents, with his mother on my left and his father on my right. We had joined arms, as if holding one another up.

As I saw the priest casting water on the coffin, I heard a voice behind me, to my left, asking, "Why are they throwing water on my body when I am standing here with you?" I turned to look, but no one was there.

That evening I lit a candle and spoke to him. It was as if his answer came in the dance of the candle flame, yet there was no breeze and no window was open. One time even the wind chimes in the room rang softly. This time there was not an audible voice as I had experienced in the church, only "thoughts."

The next evening I went into his brothers room to talk and to have someone to grieve with. But as his brother and I lay side by side talking we both noted a strange feeling, like a hot friction, emanating from the end of the bed. It was as if Philippe was present and didn't like our physical closeness. This seemed odd because nothing romantic was happening, nor did we have such intentions. It surprised us both and we came to the conclusion at the same time that I'd better get out of there. I wondered why Philippe did not understand.

I drew the conclusion that perhaps even after death, the "person" continues to grow and to learn. Just because people are dead does not mean that they come into a full understanding of everything, nor that they can read our thoughts.

The Healing Begins

I returned to my studies. This was a very difficult time. I was feeling isolated and confused. Finally I develop a full blown case of hives, all over my body. They never did find out the cause but my mother, wise as she is, thinks it was from all the grief I held inside.

Day blended into night and nothing seemed to matter. I would go to class then return to my room and as soon as the door closed, begin to cry. After a month of this, my roommate requested that I be given a room alone.

It was about this time that I went into the small town near the college and met June. She owned a clothing store and sold herb teas. She also read palms. I was browsing through the clothes when she called over to me from the counter. "Do you have a friend who wears a blue T-shirt and might have passed over?" I was stunned and replied that I do. "He is concerned about you and wants you to stop crying and get on with your life."

Upon hearing that the tears that were so near came to the surface. When I regained composure I told her that I didn't know how to get on with my life. "Why don't you meditate?" she suggested. I said that I did not know how to meditate. "Are you a Christian?" I told her I was. "Then," she said, "you know the Lord's Prayer." I offered that I say it every night. She then gave me simple advice that was to change my life in a profound way:

> "Sit in your room and begin by saying the Lord's Prayer. After the prayer, just sit quietly and try not to hold onto any thoughts. You will see that as you practice it becomes easier to sit for a longer period of time."

Sitting Still

It was amazing when I sat quietly how much noise and distractions invaded the quiet. And those that weren't there I easily conjured up. At first, to sit for 5 minutes was agonizing. I tried desperately not to itch my nose or hold onto any thought.

> *Let all your thoughts just pass by you.*
> *Do not hold onto any of them."*

June's advise was simple enough but difficult to implement at first. She was right, however; it did get easier. Pretty soon I was sitting for eight minutes then ten, then fifteen and twenty. By the second week of meditation I could sit comfortably for a half hour. And, at the end sense that "something" was happening on a "different level." I trusted Jesus to guide me into whatever "something" it was that I needed. I knew that I was learning, that roots were being set and new shoots of growth were emerging. I was willing to wait for the fruit.

I would not meditate at any specific time, just whenever I felt like it which was often. Frequently I would feel an energy pulling me from my belly into meditation. During this time I was aware of a presence in my room which was helping me in the healing process. Within that presence, I believe, was Philippe.

> *During this time I got in touch with a deep inner*
> *desire to serve.*
>
> *I wanted to serve God and thereby serve others.*

Philippe's Path Out

On the small college campus in the hills of upstate New York was a deserted chapel that had been closed down and locked up. When I felt drawn to meditate there I would approach the security guards office and they would let me in, locking the door behind me. It was a wonderful, awesome space. I would walk up the aisle and sit on the floor between the first pews, using the small, round stained glass window as a beginning focus for my prayer. Then I would close my eyes and meditate, my soul carried to places only God knows. Meditations in the chapel would last for 2 hours. I would awake from them refreshed and peaceful, with a sense that important things were taking place on the spiritual level.

One evening as I entered the chapel and heard the click of the lock behind me, I noticed the nauseous smell of funeral flowers. Chrysanthemums mixed with formaldehyde. I shuddered. Not knowing what to do, I did as usual. Upon entering the sanctuary I noticed a big ball of white light midway down the left hand side of the pews. I acknowledged it and continued down the isle to take my place on the floor.

I fell easily into the meditation and "woke" midway through to look up at the stained glass window. Something was happening. As I looked at the window I saw a stream of light come out of the window and down to where I was sitting, and sensed the image of a dove. I continued my meditation for another hour. When I awoke this time I was aware that something very special had taken place but I did not know what. It was not until a few days later, when I became aware that I no longer felt Philippe's presence in my room that I concluded that the light which emanated from the window must have served as the path he took to continue his journey. Later, when I visited his parents again, I found out that in life, Philippe had called me his angel. In death, he had been mine.

For me, this first death had opened the door of my awareness to the greater Mystery we call God. I have met death many times since. As a pastor, I have buried friends, strangers and a parent.

> ❦ *I would be lying if I said that death no longer has any sting. It does. And as long as I love life and all of God's creatures it always will. But the loss that I mourn is my own, for I know that death is not the end of the journey but a transition along the way.*

Each time I encounter death, I am more determined than ever to grow in love, to learn what it is I am here to learn and to serve with the special gifts I have been given. And more and more I take time to enjoy the Mystery called God in each and every moment.

Chapter 3

LESSONS IN THE MYSTERIOUS

A Lesson in Gifts Misused

One evening I went with June and another student to see a woman who called herself an aura reader. June warned us, "I do not know anything about this woman or how she uses her gifts. We will find out together."

And find out we did. But not as I expected. The woman was all clad in white except for a black belt at her waist. She sat on a chair in a living room and called people to stand before her where she would read their aura. I noted that it seemed odd that she found only negative stuff in all these people. I thought, "When she sees me she will find some good, because I know I am not all bad!" She turned to me and said, "Next." I stood in front of her and she read my aura, finding only negative aspects. Looking at her face, I began to see dark circles appear under her eyes and in her cheeks until she took on a demonic appearance. I could not hear what she was saying. I only saw this demon like face. I gasped and the reading was over.

On the way home June explained to us that this woman did have some gifts but she misused them. Gifts, June said, are not to be used to put people down but to help them grow. This woman was not a healer. She had her own agenda.

The Library Cat

My awareness of energy began in college when I was sitting in a library. I had just roamed the shelves filled with moldy old books. I didn't need to open them only sense their energy. I was in a mystical mood when I sat back down at a large old table. Immediately I was joined by what I assumed to be the library cat who took a place on the table above the book I brought to study.

A few minutes passed when a young man walked by, noticed the cat and reached out across me to pet it. Before he reached the cat I was aware of his energy which was erratic, not calm and smooth. His intentions were good but the cat was displeased. A hiss was followed by a scratch to the hand that reached towards it. The man cried out in surprise and left.

I sat for a moment reflecting upon what I had just witnessed. I felt the energy of the young man and decided to do a test. I reached over towards the cat and before I could touch her she warned me not to. I pulled my hand back and centered, noticing my energy until it had calmed. I reached over and stroked the cat. She purred.

I spent some time sitting there, reflecting on what I had learned. Are thoughts really an energy? Can they exist around us and effect others? Are they "catchy?" If I feel love, am I giving out an energy of love that effects others? If I feel hate or agitation, does that effect others on an energy level also? If so, then we have a great responsibility to the world.

> *We have a great responsibility to the world—not only for how we act, but also for what we think and feel beneath our actions.*

Not Doing

I leaned my back against the door and slumped to the floor, in tears. I was really alone, in a large city in Europe, and it felt like the pits. At the same time I knew that this new aloneness offered a new opportunity to meditate. It was just God and me. What would become of this? I was ready to find out.

Much of the quiet time in my room I spent in meditation and reading a book I had found called *Lamps of Fire: The Spirit of Religions*. It was the first time I really sat with Christian or other scriptures and I found the truth in them to be powerful. I also purchased a small paperback of the Upanishads and took it with me to read by the riverside. I remember spending an entire afternoon being with one Upanishad - about 3 brief phrases. Profoundly disassociating, the phrases caused me to let go of thinking and enter trans-rational states of consciousness. I was aware that this was a very important time for me on my spiritual journey and that even though I wasn't "doing" anything, a lot was happening that was affecting my very being.

As I look back I realize that this was a time when I was free to be in the moment. There were no expectations, no future goals, no one to please.

During this time of deep meditation my room was filled with a soft glowing light and I slept at night as if held in the arms of God. I was aware of having daily guidance, not only in a mystical sense but in the necessities of daily living. Once when I was standing in the bathroom guidance came in the form of an inner voice reminding me that it was time to bathe. I often sensed that I was guided to care for my physical needs because these were not that important to me at this time.

Eating Dirt—a Spiritual Lesson

To help pay my rent, I got a job baby-sitting. I would often take the child by the river and expect it to sit while I read. I loved the child but found that I had little patience for anything but a focus on my spiritual life. One day I arranged the child on the blanket and began to read. But my reading was constantly interrupted because instead of just sitting there, he ate dirt. I removed the dirt and went back to my book. but he relished in the attention he got by eating dirt, so he did it again and again. I kept having to take dirt out of his mouth. His eyes would sparkle at me while his hand clutched a piece of dirt placed precariously near his mouth.

The final time he would not let me remove the dirt. So I took three fingers and tapped his cheek, hoping he would open his mouth. He didn't. I tapped harder, and made a small sound. The sound surprised me and, struck with sudden guilt, I wondered if I had tapped him too hard. He was surprised too but didn't cry. I picked him up and gave him lots of attention — which was all he seeking in the first place. Then I noticed a mark on his soft, rosy cheeks, left by my fingers.

When I took him home to his parents they questioned me about the mark. I tried to weasel out of it, realizing that this did not look good. I felt shame and guilt and didn't know how to explain it to them. Needless to say, I was fired.

The guilt and shame have lasted even to this day. In fact, I have inserted this passage during early editing work because it makes an important statement about the spiritual journey. I may have needed to simply be in retreat and do nothing else. But how often is that possible? The truth of the matter is that the child was my path when I was with the child. And it was a mistake to move away from the child by trying to read on our walks. Or to see the child and the spiritual path as separate. Our needs were the same. Companionship, love, simplicity. He needed to be cared for and I needed emotional growth. I could have found what I needed by getting out of the way and experiencing the path of caring. But I did not know that.

How often I see parents, partners and pet owners treat their spiritual path as separate from their children, partners and pets. When we stop fighting their needs and get out of the way we see that truly loving and caring for them in this moment is what we need for our own growth and wellness. Then the conflict is truly resolved. This goes beyond duality of "my need versus theirs". And it's not about staying in an abusive relationship or not taking time for oneself. It's deeper than that.

> *Those things which are a thorn in our side have the most to teach us about our ego's resistance to the movements of God in the present moment.*

I was spiritually connected by my reading. I didn't realize I could have been just as connected by attending to the needs of a rosy cheeked, dirt eating child.

My much needed lesson would come years later with a loving, earthy husband and two wonderful, demanding dogs who tend not to be as patient or as subtle about their needs as the little child.

> *Sometimes we forget that we are human for a reason, and each and every moment here on earth is a perfect opportunity to fulfill that reason.*

Vision of Christ

One day the two young women next door invited me up to their apartment. I accepted. Their motivation soon became clear when they announced, "We want to tell you about Jesus."

This seemed odd but I went along. Not feeling comfortable in their space, I suggested, "Let's go for a walk by the river." As we were walking and the young woman was telling me about Jesus I had a strong thought, "Why is she telling me about myself? Does she not know who I am?"

> *A focus on doctrine all too often separates us from the very experience of the holy we are professing.*

Then came the vision. I looked down at my feet and instead of seeing jeans and shoes I saw a robe and sandals. It was the first time that I was aware I had "put on Christ," literally. The event seemed odd and yet I was aware that Jesus is an experience, not of doctrine as the women were teaching, but of the sacredness in life to which we are all connected. It taught me that people can profess religion on an intellectual level and be totally unaware of the sacredness present in that very moment when it does not correspond with their doctrine or belief system.

> *Could the changes that are triggered within us when we have a religious experience of Jesus, Buddha or Mohammed etc. be but a response to the mirror they serve of the archetypal divine nature within our very selves? Could it be that the holy figures help to burn away the clutter and help to get us in touch with our inner divinity— with who we really are?*

The Leaves of the Peach Tree Will Heal You

I enjoyed walking the streets of this small European town in which I lived.

> *The gentle summer breeze would rustle through the trees and bless all that it touched.*
> *Life seemed very sacred and I did, too.*

One day I entered a strange old book store. I found a Bible that I wanted but I only had a dollar. When I took it to the elderly man at the counter to ask how much it cost, he looked kindly at me and asked, "How much do you have?" I told him, "One dollar." He said, "That is exactly how much it costs." I returned home with my find and put it on the table. I had not yet opened it because I was reading scripture from the other books.

A few days later, I passed by a street theater performance in a part of town not very familiar to me. Suddenly, out of the blue, one of the players came up to me and held out a small green army tin in his hand. "Take these," he said. "They are peach tree leaves and someday you might need them." Somewhat dumbfounded, I accepted the gift. When I got home I put the mysterious tin all the way to the back of the shelf and forgot about it.

A couple of weeks later I was feeling strange. Something was not right and I wondered if I was getting sick. As I sat in my room, I reached over and picked up the Bible that had been laying on the table. I opened to what I now realize was some place in the Old Testament. My eyes caught a passage in the lower left hand corner because it was highlighted with light. The light seemed to come from behind and surround these words: "The leaves of the peach tree will heal you." I remembered the tin I had been given and recovered it from the back of the shelf. I boiled some of the leaves, ate them and lay down. When I awoke I felt different and good. I was healed.

Years later, when I went to seminary I opened the biggest concordance I could find and looked for the words I had read that day. They are not in the Bible.

"Reading" Energy

One day I was invited to an informal gathering. I noticed that a few were off to the side trying to raise a person with one finger. It's a little party game people liked to play that is supposed to prove that if a persons spirit leaves their body, or they are under the suggestion that they are very light, the body becomes lighter and can be picked up easily with four people using only one or two fingers. Some of the others had gathered around and were poo-pooing the idea. I didn't have an opinion one way or the other. What did affect me however was that they seemed to be seeking proof of the spirit. Proof that we are more than what we can see and touch.

Upon that realization a change come over me and I felt that familiar pull that guided me to invite the group to sit in a circle around me. There, I asked them to hand an object to me, one at a time, always given to me by the same person. I did not know who owned the object as I sat with my eyes closed. When I received it I "read" the energy, a psychic tool known as psychometry which June had taught me. I came up with names of places, persons, horses, events, illnesses etc. which still held energy for that person. Then, to give it back to the right person, I would simply match the energy in the object to the energy of a person in the circle.

I had practiced psychometry while in college and played around with it once in a while after that. June had said that most everyone can do it with practice. The practice is necessary to filter out one's own thoughts from what comes from the object.

All things hold and give off energy.
We are in touch with this every day when we
become aware of how a place, person, animal or
object feels to us.

When I held an object to my forehead, I was aware of the energy as different from my own. The last object I held and began to "read" had such erratic, scattered energy that it made me dizzy and I had to take it away before I could read it. After collecting and centering my own energy I started with it again. Then, without hesitation, I handed it back to the person with the same erratic and scattered energy, saying, "This is yours!"

A Strange Visit

We had an old cabin situated on 30 acres of pine and maple forest. In front of the cabin was a beautiful small lake. I spent weeks at a time in "God's country." The summers were perfect for lying on the cement slab by the lake wearing nothing but what God gave me. Early mornings and evenings would require a small fire in the wood stove. Though there were mosquitoes in abundance, by fall most of them were gone and walks in the woods were very invigorating. I spent most of my time walking the dogs, doing art work, reading *Lamps of Fire* and meditating. It was a good time just to Be and it never occurred to me that anyone would violate this time.

My great aunt always warned me to be careful of bears around the camp. But bears were not the problem. The danger was more of the human type. One quiet evening as I sat by the wood stove deep in contemplation the silence was interrupted by the sound of an approaching car. I got up to look out the window and I could see the headlights coming towards the cabin. It was unusual for anyone to accidentally drive to the cabin. It was not clearly marked. Whoever it was must know that I am here and they must have come for a reason. Fear filled my mind. Did someone see me naked by the lake? Have people been hanging around unbeknownst to me? Was I in danger? Voices of panic screamed out from inside of me, "Lock the windows, bar the door!" But the windows did not lock and anyone who was strong and determined enough could easily enter.

Suddenly I heard another voice. It was different. This was not the voice of panic or fear. The words were clear, the voice was authoritative, calm and compassionate. It was as if a man was standing by my left side. The words were few: "It's o.k., I'm with you."

I did not know who spoke but the fear and panic left and it was as if I knew what to do. I waited by the door until the man approached. I didn't know him. He was a young bearded man in his late 20's or mid 30's, with a six-pack of beer in his right hand. "I thought we could talk," I remember him saying. I invited him in and we sat at my grandfather's library table. We each opened a beer and I took a sip then set it down. I remember that our conversation turned to God. After that I remember nothing.

An hour later the conversation was over and I regained full consciousness. We were sitting just as we had begun. The man got up to leave saying, "Wow! No one's ever talked to me like that." Of course, I had no idea what was said but I trusted it was what God knew he needed to hear. As I closed the screen door behind him he said, "I'll be back." I smiled and waved good-bye but I knew he would not return. There was no reason. The "test" was over. What test it was I have no idea, but I am grateful for the results.

Danny

Danny, I was told, had emotional problems and had tried to stab his mother. I had never met Danny before and didn't think much about it.

One day I accompanied my parents on a visit to the home of Danny and his parents. Danny and I quickly struck up a conversation about the book he was reading, *Sidhartha*. Danny was interested in religion and suggested we continue the conversation in his room, for more privacy. There he began to tell me about how scared he was. He would have terrible dreams and sometimes feared that evil spirits were lurking in his closet. It must have been awful to live that way.

As I listened, Danny then told me about how cool it was to have power. For instance, he said, as he was riding his bike down the street, he would put out his hand and people would jump back as if hit by some blow of energy. It was not hard to see the simple truth that as long as he used this power in a negative manner, he would also be haunted by it. I told him so and suggested that he choose what he wanted. Either he could have power and be possessed by it or he could reject it and live in peace.

As we were talking I was aware that light from my 3rd eye was being sent out to Danny. I let this continue for the duration of the conversation, thinking nothing about it. Then Danny asked me, "What does it mean when there is a tunnel of white light?" "What do you mean?" I asked him. "Well" Danny said, "I see a tunnel of white light between us." "Danny," I said, somewhat surprised, "You have some wonderful gifts, but you have to choose how you will use them."

Three days later the phone rang. It was Danny's mother. While on the phone with her my mom turned to me and asked, "What were you doing with Danny the other night?" I asked her why she wanted to know. My mother asked that question of Danny's mom and replied back to me that "Danny has been different since that night. He has been more calm." I was glad to hear that but simply offered back that we had just talked. What else could I say?

Chapter 4

PEACE CORPS KOREA

Decision to Join the Peace Corps

During my last year at Michigan State I applied to the Peace Corps. I had wanted to go to Zimbabwe because I was interested in political developments within the country and with South Africa. But no jobs in Zimbabwe were offered. Instead, I received a call from Washington DC asking if I wanted to go to Swaziland and work as a slaughter house inspector. I mentioned that it might be a difficult position for me since I am a vegetarian, so the offer was retracted.

A few weeks later I received another offer asking if I wanted to go to Korea and work as a leprosy health care worker. The offer was not what I had expected and I needed a few days to reflect. Something stirred in me. I began to see it not so much as offering a political lesson, but rather a spiritual one. Could I see beneath a person's skin into the soul?

The small town where I would be working was in the mid section of the country. As the only American in the area, I made every effort to blend into Korean life and culture as much as possible. During this time I got to know my health center co-worker, a dear man who had great respect for the villagers.

One day, on a visit with my co-worker to the resettlement village, the village leader took us for a hike up the narrow dirt road near some houses set into the side of the mountain. It was a high area of the village and there, looking over the village and surrounding mountains, he asked me if I would like to live there. There was no doubt in my mind. "Yes," I said in Korean, nodding my head as tears welled up in my eyes. Never had I seen a lovelier place.

Over the years the village has grown and that place where we stood is no longer as lovely as it once was. But the people still are wonderful, and the village leader, now living in a large city, is still the wise and compassionate man I knew him to be on that visit when he showed me the village and asked if I wanted to make this my home.

Carbon Monoxide Poisoning

In our early training, the Peace Corps warned us of carbon monoxide poisoning that occurs from the commonly used charcoal heaters. More than few, living off base had been killed in their sleep by carbon monoxide.

I seem to have forgotten this lesson when I got fed up with being cold one winter and bought a charcoal heater for my small room. I put plastic over the windows and had things pretty well sealed up. Boy did it get warm! No more sleeping with hat and mittens.

One night, as I was sleeping peacefully with my cat, a presence woke me up. I still don't know who it was. I don't recall seeing her. It seemed angelic and her message was, "Wake up and get out of the room."

So I woke up and went into the meeting hall adjacent to my room. As soon as I opened the door, I passed out. I recovered consciousness to find myself wedged up against the speaker system, having wet my pants. I went to the window and opened it to get some fresh air, having figured out what had probably happened. I went back and retrieved my cat and mattress and laid them in the meeting room. I got the cat's box as well because I was feeling sick. Then, cat and self all safe, I went back to sleep.

Some villagers walking by saw me asleep in the meeting room and went to inform my village sister and her husband. They came to check on me and graciously invited me to stay at their house for a few days while recovering.

It is a miracle that I did not die in my sleep. I figured I had something more to learn and something to complete. My time to die had not yet come.

Looking back, it is good that I did not die. Not only would it have been a tremendous hardship for my parents and the Peace Corp program, but a terrible burden on the villagers, a people I had grown to love.

> *For everything there is a season, and a time for every matter under heaven: a time to be born and a time to die ....*
>
> Ecclesiastes 3:1-2a

A Time to Die

It was not my time to die but it was Mr. Kim's time. Mr. Kim was a lovely man in his late sixties who had contracted spinal meningitis. My first visit to his house came when his neighbors told me that he was sick and asked if I would check on him. He was very sick and had not yet seen a doctor. Many of the villagers hesitated to get medical care because they felt ostracised by the uninformed towns people and health workers who were afraid of catching leprosy. I arranged for the health center doctor to come to the village and he suggested that Mr. Kim go to the local hospital for further tests.

I was delighted to be able to 'make a difference', and perhaps prolong or even save this man's life. Day after day I sat by his bedside in the hospital, determined not to have him miss out on any modern health care.

One day, after about two weeks of numerous tests and antibiotic drugs, Mr. Kim looked up at me from his bed on the floor and said,

"I appreciate all that you have done but now I would like to go home to die."

I was shocked; taken aback by the possibility that he had swallowed all those drugs and endured all the procedures and hardship simply to please me and, perhaps, a vague hope of recovery. Humbled by this realization, I said,

"I understand, Mr. Kim. Would you please do me a small favor? When you see Jesus, would you please tell him that I said hello and we are doing our best?" He assured me he would.

Mr. Kim died in his home about a week later. I was honored with an invitation to see his wrapped body and grieve with his wife, then attend the village funeral and feast.

I had thought I was patiently holding Mr. Kim's hand on his deathbed. Now I realized that he had held mine just as patiently while I grappled with my own resistance to death. I will never forget Mr. Kim for teaching me that there is a time to live and there is a time to let go and die.

Political Unrest

Oddly enough, accepting and loving people who have a disease and are living in poverty was not the most difficult lesson for me. That came easily. I enjoyed making home visits, doing physical therapy and teaching English and sanitation. I loved the people. I loved our small mountain village.

The stress I felt was political. When I went to the country in 1979 the somewhat benevolent military dictatorship of Park Chung He was still in place, going on twenty some years. During his rule there had been tremendous industrial developments but few in terms of human rights and self determination. If people wanted to talk politics, say at the local cafe, they would lower their voice and turn nervously to see who might be an under cover policeman. It was a nation living in fear. The Korean governments methods of repressing news within the country began to wear on me. My Newsweek was censored and any news of communist North Korea was blacked out and pictures of the N. Korean dictator actually cut out!

Whenever the South Korean students would demonstrate for democracy, the government would try to suppress the news of the demonstration and the number of injuries by putting news of a captured North Korean spy on the front page of the newspaper. Many of the spies had been caught months earlier. The government was just waiting to use it for damage control. Most news got around by word of mouth. Someone who was there told someone else etc. It wasn't very reliable but it seemed better than governmental controlled sources such as the radio, television or newspapers.

I found something very disabling about the suppression of truth and something very hopeful about a people who had to have tremendous courage to use their voice. It was as if the government didn't believe in their people's ability to determine their own lives. I learned first hand how abusive power can be and how it can disable the lives of others.

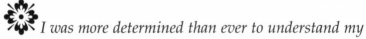

I was more determined than ever to understand my own use of personal power, and committed myself to the process of empowering and believing in others.

Books in Cages and Hope Dashed

One afternoon I visited the local library and discovered that all the books were in metal cages, inaccessible unless accompanied by someone with a key, I took action. I began to write into the national newspaper to an English column called "My Turn." I wrote about the library situation then wrote stories which were allegories about the political situation.

An industrialist from Seoul read the article and got in touch with me. He said he wanted to help create an open library and was willing to donate towards the cause. With a local Korean friend who knew some English, I approached the director of education. The director indicated an interest in the project. We were to go ahead and raise the funds and they would expand the library. Something did not fit in the picture and my Korean friend could not get the director to confirm that the books would not be locked up but on open shelves. In Korea a yes can mean no and my friend was discerning that the director's yes was most likely no.

When it came time to hand over the money we raised, I hesitated. We still didn't have a promise that the books would be on open shelves. The director indicated that he was concerned about theft, and therefore the books had to remain under lock and key. We tried to propose solutions but were not making progress. The language and cultural barriers were not helping. I was in over my head.

Then one day the village leader asked me to move forward and give the money to the educational director. I explained that the money would not be used for its purpose and this was not fair to the students or the industrialist who helped raise it. But the village leader explained that not to give the money would hurt our village and the chances of our children entering the schools.

I felt used, caught in a cultural system that didn't make sense and betrayed by the educational director who knew what he was planning all along. I apologized to the industrialist about the situation and asked what he wanted to do. He said that the only option was to hand the money over and hope that one day the library will be truly open. We decided not to attend any ceremony being held and not play into any more of the educational director's game than necessary. For the director, his actions were simply a cultural way of life and I doubt that he saw them as intentionally deceptive.

Assassination

In 1980 Dictator Park was assassinated. In a way, this was a time of hope. There was the possibility for change. A Mr. Roh, a supposedly non military man was chosen to fill in for Park. The country was on edge. I was hopeful and wrote a number of stories. One story was about a people who decided to stop a ritual of beating themselves and once they got through the initial headache, found out that it was OK, even wonderful not to beat themselves.

This story never got to the newspaper office. In fact, it was at this time that the US. government suggested to the head of the Peace Corps Korea that my writing was inflammatory, and seditious. I was offered a choice — stay and shut up or continue to write and leave.

As it turned out, I did not have to work too hard on my answer. Roh did not last long in office. The military was anxious to be back in power. The new dictator by coup d'état was Chun Do Wan. I was in Seoul at the time. You would not believe the number of tanks in the street. And one, unfortunately was sitting right outside the newspaper office.

The Kwang-Ju Uprising, Death and Grief for Korea

> ॐ *In my garden what do I see—*
> *a bird high up in a cherry tree.*
> *A pine tree tall whose needles fall,*
> *and make a bed for blossoms dead.*

Dominance, power, oppression. Fear, helplessness, hate. The hope the country felt was shattered and in Kwang Ju the people took to the streets. Men, women, teenagers and children. I'm told that it began as an angry but nonviolent demonstration. I'll never know what really happened in Kwang Ju. I wasn't there. Soon after the riot broke out the Peace Corps office in Seoul called. I was making my rounds in a neighboring village and did not get back till around eight in the evening. Waiting for me was a message: I was to catch the next train to Seoul.

It turns out that the South Korean government was taking some of their most deadliest trained, most amoral soldiers (known as "snake eyes") off the DMZ to fight the people demonstrating in Kwang Ju. This can only be done with U.S. approval since our two countries patrol the DMZ together. Thus the call. The US. must have known that what was going to take place would be a bloody awful atrocity. And it was. The air was filled with the cries of people who had left their homes that day, never to return. The two Peace Corps members who had gotten stuck in the city reported taking wounded to the hospitals and finding them packed full of wounded and dying. Some say that the helicopters shot at unarmed civilians from the sky. Others reported that one of the snake eyes had bayoneted a pregnant woman and ripped out her fetus.

For the next few weeks families lived in terror that their college aged children would be "reported" as being at the demonstration and taken from their home to be tortured. Their fear was valid, for each person tortured was to "report" the names of others. Pictures circulated of dead young men in coffins, their thumbs tied together with wire.

The numbers of people killed were high. The word on the street was two thousand; the government reported only two hundred. The fact that the South Korean government lied was no surprise. What did surprise me was how little of all this reached the American public. Congress, on the other hand, got first hand information from the two Peace Corps volunteers in Kwang-Ju, who were taking people to the hospital. Word was that they had been able to catch some of the incident on film. And for this reason, the the U.S. government sent them immediately to Washington and home. Obviously, there was a lot they could share with Congress. And more obvious, their lives were at risk if they stayed in Korea.

When I returned to the states, at the end of my service, I called the office of a senator who I had met while he toured a resettlement village. The senator was not in so an aid took my call. I voiced my concern over the situation in Korea. I doubted that I had much effect.

One evening, fourteen years later, I just happened to turn on the television to a public broadcasting station program. That night, for the first time, I saw the film footage of the Kwang-Ju incident.

Loving the Enemy

Back at the village I seethed with hatred and rage. I cut out a picture of Chun Do Wan and threw a homemade dart at it. I hated the man. I hated the government. I hated the soldiers, I hated my own country for supporting such outrage and then saying very little about it back home.

> ❧ *Pretty soon, I realized I was being consumed with hate. I had become possessed by the enemy because I held on to their weapon of choice. I began to ask myself, "What happened to love?" Is there not some way that I could love my enemy?*

After all, the cat in the library had taught me that thoughts are energy. Was I helping myself or anyone else by sending out hate? Could I not see the soul of the soldier?

I vividly recall one day when I was back in Seoul. I was walking down the street praying: "Please Jesus help me feel love." I would walk about 3 steps in love and felt hate again for 5 steps. Again I would pray and so on until the feeling of love lasted longer than hate. As I waited for a bus, I decided that if I saw a soldier, I would send to him energy of love and see what happened.

The bus arrived and as I stepped on I told the bus girl where I needed to get off. Standing in front of where I was sitting was a soldier. Here was my opportunity and my challenge. My first feelings for him were not love. So I prayed. "God, if it be your will, help me to feel love for this soldier." And amazingly enough I did. Then I felt an inner challenge to reach out to him and say hello. But I apologized saying I wasn't ready to go that far yet. So I just sat there, sending out waves of love. And who was more surprised then me when the soldier turned around, gently touched my arm and as he departed said, "Your stop is the next one after mine."

Monk's Hill

Every so often I would make a pilgrimage to a small Buddhist temple on the outskirts of town. A bus would let me off at the base of the hill and I would climb for about a half hour before arriving at the temple. There, I was greeted by a middle aged monk and an elderly woman. Though we could hardly communicate, we enjoyed each other's company. I would be welcomed and shown a room where I could spend the night. They always seemed delighted to have a visitor and I was refreshed by the sacredness of their mountain home.

One late afternoon I was visiting with them and asked to use the bathroom. They pointed to the path around the house. I followed the path to come to a shoulder height straw and mud wall supported by four poles. The back and sides were sheltered for privacy and the fourth side opened to a majestic view of the mountain range. It was the most primitive outhouse I'd ever seen, with a view the rich would die for.

Greeting me near the earthen hole was the biggest and fattest toad I had ever seen. He was at least seven inches tall and six inches in circumference. He was there catching the flies that would hatch from the larva in the waste in the hole. Now that's a fresh catch! I waited a moment for the resourceful creature to give up his watch over the hole and took my turn. As I was making my offering to the earth, I was awed by the magnificence of the mountain range. The beauty. The simplicity. Timeless. Pure. Until the deafening roar of a military spy plane overhead shattered the silence. Suddenly I was caught between two worlds. It was the strangest most disassociating feeling I've ever had.

One day I went to Monk's Hill only to find that neither the monk nor the elderly woman was there. I decided to meditate and felt drawn to the top of a ledge higher up the mountain. Leading to the ledge were little chiseled indentations, barely big enough for a foot. I had on my flip flops (the only sandal I could find close to my size) and "scaled" the ledge thinking that mom would have a fit if she could see me now.

At the top of the ledge was a small pine tree and a perfect place to sit and meditate. The spot overlooked the mountain range; a more beautiful, awesome place I have never seen. It could not have been more than a minute or two after I sat down that I was deep in a meditation which lasted perhaps an hour. As the meditation period was coming to a close I suddenly became aware that I had become a part of the mist over the mountains. I was the mist. I was the primal energy of life. There was no 'me' separate from this. The next thing I knew I heard a bird sing. The song came from me. Then it came from the bird and the bird was separate from me and I awoke.

I was descending the hill to go back to my village when I encountered the monk. He asked me to stay. But I said that I must go and I continued my descent. This was my last visit to Monk's Hill.

Often, now, when I sit in meditation, I feel a closeness with the monk and a tenderness for him, as each of us, in our sacred places, becomes one with all that is.

> *Were there more love in me, I would disappear into the mountain mist — from whence I came.*

The Imperfect Christian Community

As with any human endeavor, Christian communities have been imperfect since they began. Indeed, even the community of disciples in the time of Jesus had their short comings. That's just the way it is. And any time someone tries to make them "perfect" we end up with some weird cult.

The village I was living in was a Christian village. It had a small church where the people worshipped daily at 5am, Wed. and Sat. pm and Sun. am. If worship could make us holy, these people were saints. And yet, even saints have their faults. So it was in this village that I decided to claim the Christian community as my own. After all, I was not perfect, either.

> *Maybe God is simply asking us to grow, to Be, and along the way, to love one another.*

Although I am open to the truth revealed in many sacred writings, I have found Biblical texts to be especially meaningful. But I never was aware of the experience of Christian community. Indeed, it was in the context of the village community that the words of Paul to the newly formed Christian communities became alive. And, it was the constant badgering of the villagers asking me, "Are you a Christian?" that brought me to the point of claiming the Christian community as my own.

> Knowing in my heart that God is and always will be more than any religious institution can define or claim.

The problem for them was that they knew I meditated and at that time in Korea, to meditate meant you are a Buddhist. There were clear cut lines for everything it seemed, and I just didn't fit in any category. It puzzled me that they would not just assume that I was a Christian based upon my actions. And once I asked them if I appeared to be a Christian to them. In my heart there was never any question.

> So often we place more importance on what we confess than on how we live.

Claiming my Christianity in the context of Christian community however, helped open the way for a career in ministry.

I made friends with a young man in the village named Youngman. His name means "a thousand different ways to go in life". One evening on a walk together I asked him what he wanted to do with his life. He told me he had always wanted to be a minister. Suddenly I thought, "I already am. This is what I am doing."

There didn't seem to be many other options for living in the sacred. It couldn't be a secondary thing for me. It is who I am and it had to be what I do.

A few months later, as our friendship grew, we discussed the option of marriage.

To Wed or Not to Wed

In many ways it was a sense of common vocation which urged me to ask him if he wanted to marry. More than that though it was the fact that, in spite of the language barrier, we enjoyed each others company and had many deep conversations on spirituality and life. It was clear that if he was going to be a minister, it would be best to leave the country in order to get the education he needed. Korea provided few second chances at that time and, since he left school to work at the age of fourteen, he would need to make up for lost time and opportunity.

I clearly remember my inner dialogue over the question of marriage. I was choosing between getting married or not getting married at all. Either seemed a feasible option and either offered different opportunities.

Having almost killed myself the previous winter, and feeling like a self imposed martyr for working over the Christmas holiday, I decided to return to the States for a month. This trip home would give me the opportunity to be with the idea of marriage in my own cultural context and to get away from the pressures Koreans put on women to marry by the age of twenty seven.

But being back in the States did not make my decision about marriage any clearer. In fact I realized that I would be as happy not married as married. It was really my choice and either way would be OK. This internal realization was mirrored by my parents who said the same thing.

I left the States deciding to go ahead with our plans to marry.

Fifteen years later I can say that our decision to marry must have come from a much deeper place than emotional attachment or rational thought. And it is from that deeper place that we learned to adjust and grow into life together. In the ensuing years I have been blown away by how much we have grown to love each other and come to appreciate and respect our differences while relishing our similarities and retaining a sense of humor about it all.

> *It is the steadfast framework of our commitment to our relationship which has pulled us through changes and hard times over the years. It is that same steadfastness which also has given us the framework within which to work out our conflicts and grow, knowing that come thick or thin, we are in this together.*

A Village Wedding

My husband and I were married in the village at the church. It was a time of great preparation and excitement. Youngman's parents and their friends were involved in the preparation and the entire village was at the celebration. Youngman looked handsome in his suit and the bowl hair cut I had given him. I had my hair permed at a shop in town and it looked pretty awful. I was dressed by my mother in-law, her close friend and my village sister. I wore a traditional Korean wedding dress, a gift from my in-laws. I remember that my village sister was so busy in the preparations she hadn't had time to change out of her work clothes.

People often ask if my parents were present. We decided that the twenty-one hour flight over and the food and living conditions would cause more hardship then it was worth. Instead, my parents wanted to have a party for us on our return. As a result, our parents have never met, although they have exchanged translated letters. So I was honored when the village leader offered to stand in place of my father and walk me down the isle.

It was a two hour service with everyone and his brother speaking. I am told that a number of government officials spoke. All I knew was that I had on a pair of traditional narrow rubber shoes and I have a wide foot. The pain was increasing until relief came when someone said to me,"Say 'I do.'" I did and to this day I tease my husband by asking, "Did I say 'I do' to *that?*"

The village had prepared a wonderful feast which we enjoyed after the wedding. It was very special for us to be married in the village and it was good for the village as well, since our wedding made the national TV news. In Seoul, people who would avoid a person from a leprosy resettlement village for fear of the disease, were coming up to shake the hand of my husband, who was now a celebrity.

A Honeymoon of Strawberries and a Mating Dance

We decided to take our honeymoon trip to the southern So Ruk Island where my husband spent ten years of his childhood. We stayed at the coast for our first night and would go over to the island the next day.

Our first evening was memorable. We had bought some local strawberries and washed them with tap water. Youngman had diarrhea for a few hours. I was OK. That evening he was in much better shape and being in a good mood, he did what I call an improvisational mating dance. I was already lying in the traditional Korean bed, on the floor, somewhat stunned by his antics. Without thinking, I had placed my eye glasses within reach, just above the pillow, on the floor, as I always did. The reader can probably guess what happened. At one point in the mating dance Youngman's foot landed on my glasses. Crack!! For the next fifteen years, he would remind me to put my glasses in a safe place when I took them off.

When I became ordained as a pastor I met with couples for premarital counseling and wedding planning. With those who were overly concerned with having every little detail be 'perfect,' I would share my own wedding and honeymoon experience and we would have a good laugh.

Vacation on the Leprosy Island

I found a way to fix the glasses so that they could be worn and the next day we headed out to the island.The island beaches have always been a vacation spot for those able to afford such luxuries. It was also the sight of the leprosy sanatorium where my mother-in-law was placed during her illness. Her husband, Youngman's biological father, divorced her when she became sick. This was common at the time, although women who did not have the disease tended to stay with their husbands.

At the time of the move, Youngman was only five years old. The doctors and authorities were not allowing children to remain with their parents for fear that the children would contact the disease—something they really didn't know much about at that time. So the children were forced to live in an orphanage having only non contact, supervised group visits with their parents. Youngman recalls the stress of these visits as parents cried at seeing their children and were unable to touch, being separated by a fence.

I always thought it a strange mix. An extremely poor leprosy colony in one spot and a vacation resort for doctors and wealthy friends on the beach nearby. The picture was made even more stark as Youngman reported that he and some of the other children would go to the beach at night and eat the watermelon rinds that were thrown on the beach by the vacationers. I have encouraged him to write his story and someday, when he is ready, he just may.

So here we were. On vacation ourselves, returning to the spot where Youngman had many memories. There were not many left in the leprosy colony. Only a few people who had been so poor and deformed by the disease that they choose not to or could not leave.

We visited with those who remain behind. Some of these kind people had cared for Youngman after his mother had remarried and gone with her husband to find a home for the family at a resettlement village on the mainland.

This beautiful island, my home for eight years. I recognize the torn down site where long ago stood a wooden structure safeguarding one hundred of us—children of leprosy patients.

The rusty old wire fence brings back yesterday's sorrow, loneliness, sadness and hunger.

I think of my friends who are gone, vanished without a trace, as if they wanted to forget their past.

I recognize old deformed faces that have lived here for more than forty years—prisoners, caged animals with no way out.

I see their faces smiling as they see me and my new foreign wife. Calling my name with joy and excitement, they touch us again and again, enjoying rare outside human contact.

I'm a hero of some sort, today.

Youngman Chai

Part Two

Savoring

Chapter 5

GIFTS AND GROWING EDGES

Entering Open Arms

Our plane landed in the States and my parents met us at the airport. This was the first time they had seen my new husband. I remember my father greeted us first and I noticed my mother's eyes checking Youngman up and down before she gave him a big hug—a surprise to him as Koreans don't hug. But to me the hug was a relief and a testament to the unconditional love I had come to appreciate in my parents.

I remember their first male bonding ritual. It was after dinner and Dad suggested they go down stairs to the basement to play ping pong. Now, realize that any communication they had for the first few months was only through me unless they used international hand gestures. My concern for their ability to communicate soon diminished with the sound of roaring laughter and taunts coming from the basement. I was astonished that my husband was so competitive. My Dad was delighted.

Discovering My Leadership Qualities

After a few months, my husband's competitiveness began to pay off as he began working in my father's factory. In spite of language barriers, he was, Dad often said, one of the best workers.

I found a job coordinating in-home services for the elderly. I supervised a staff of five and made home visits. We also provided respite for those caring for their parents in their homes.

This was the first job I had where I supervised others and it brought out a lot of my latent leadership skills. Oddly enough, these began to emerge during the interview process.

The person interviewing me was the one whose job I would be taking over. She was leaving the agency and had a lot to say about who would replace her. This seemed odd to me at the time. The interview took place in her office, a small windowless room in the back of an old building. She smoked incessantly. Her mannerisms and description of the agency seemed uncooperative and rigid. I sensed that there was not a lot of good feeling between her and the director of the agency. And I sensed that her relationship with the staff was authoritarian.

Midway through the interview, I began to get hot flashes as if I were coming down with a bad case of the flu. I mentioned this and we wrapped up the interview. As soon as I got outside into the fresh air, I noted with surprise that I felt fine. I went over to the building next door to speak with the director. She seemed like a competent, kind and straight forward professional. I decided to be honest and straight forward with her. So I said, "I am interested in the job but will only take it if you and I can work together. I will not perpetuate the former tension, ill feelings and lack of cooperation I sense pervades the agency." She agreed with a sense of relief.

 I had honored my truth and received hers in return.

My leadership method was in sharp contrast to that of the former coordinator. I had an opportunity to be an agent of empowerment where there had previously been repression. The most obvious example of this came when I gathered the staff of five together for a meeting to discuss how things were going. They were amazed when I asked them to talk about the clients. The former coordinator, they said, made it clear that any talk about clients was considered gossip. They seemed afraid so I said I would check it out with the director. They were bewildered that I would do that as the former coordinator didn't seem to involve the director in any of the in-home staff business.

Soon, in an atmosphere of confidentiality, respect and support, they shared their concerns, joys and struggles. Their sense of isolation and being overwhelmed with the needs of clients was overcome by a sense of love, support and professionalism. In response to their desire to learn to "take off the work coat" at the end of the day and not wake up at night worrying about their clients, I brought in a wonderful counselor from County Mental Health to join us once a month. This proved to be beneficial. The team work and healing this brought our staff, and the better quality of service our clients received brought me great satisfaction.

> *If our goal is to live our lives aligned with our soul, then we can no longer blindly adopt the diagnosis and dogma of the medical and religious establishments which ignore the wisdom of our souls.*

Late one day, the phone rang and an anxious, distraught and depressed voice threatened: "I think I'm going to kill myself."

The voice belonged to a woman I'll call Ruth, who was caring for her mother. I managed to contact a local mental health worker who offered to see Ruth after hours. I also arranged the mental health appointment for Ruth and set up a home visit the next day to evaluate the needs of her and her mother and arrange a respite care schedule for her. By the time I made the home visit, Ruth had seen the mental health professional and had scheduled another visit with him.

While talking in the kitchen, I found out that Ruth drank a couple of pots of coffee a day. I mentioned that excess coffee leads to greater feelings of anxiety and suggested that she cut back. She then took me to meet her bedridden mother. Their relationship was tense and as I recall the mother was verbally abusive. I arranged to have our staff come into the home so Ruth could have some time of her own away from her mother. It seemed to me that the combination of counseling, better self care and time on her own would benefit both Ruth and her mother.

In a routine follow up, however, Ruth shared with me that she had been to see her doctor who told her that she did not need mental health care, she just needed some valium! After that I knew that not much would change for Ruth or her mother.

In this job I learned that those of us who are given positions of authority in an organization have a tremendous influence on how, why and if people work together, and in what kind of atmosphere the work gets done. Years later, I would see the effects of fearful leadership and decision making in church and governmental institutions as well as in the lives of individuals.

As I look back, I see that my in-home services work set a base of confidence in the power of love.

I enjoyed this job and was sorry to leave it when I was accepted into seminary.

---

cho *Intellectual, outer knowledge must be balanced with inner wisdom and experience.*

Chapter 6

SEMINARY

We Don't Talk About That Here

When I arrived at seminary I was anxious to share my experiences of God and to discover how they fit into the Christian context. What I found out was that these experiences of the mystical, spiritual presence of God were something that may indeed be "real" but one doesn't talk about them.

Of course, that is like telling a puppy not to play or a horse not to run or an angel not to fly. So I chose whom I told and when. I shared a bit here and there, and when I did, I found out that some others have had similar experiences that they too needed to share.

Seminary was a good time for me because my experience of God was now being balanced with intellectual understanding. I understood in the context of experience. I found new affirmation and energy in seminary.

Although I felt affirmed, I also knew that my experiences made me different from many of the seminarians who came to seminary looking for the experience of God only to find an intellectually built waste land. I came with experience seeking the Biblical and intellectual aspect and found the grounds rich and sacred.

I often had a sense of the spirit "bubbling up" from inside and flowing out. So much so that one day I could not contain it, got up from my grandfather's library table, stood up on the sofa back and wrote PRAISE GOD on the wall. The next day, a class on spirituality was meeting in my apartment (it was the only class on spirituality offered at our seminary). I tried to explain why the words were there but the explanation fell short of the experience. It would not be the first time that my colleagues would look at me with a "questionably odd" glance.

Our spirituality professor had asked us to keep a journal during the duration of the class. I however have never been prone to write on a daily basis. Because my soul often communicates visually I hold very sacred what is written. I can only write from my soul, especially if it is a journal - writings from my deepest space and what I put in a sacred journal just comes as gift from up out of the mysterious depths.

So I did not do the assignment. Instead, I reflected on this and wrote a poem instead:

> *All things are resolved*
> *and there is from the clatter of thoughts — a*
> *silence,*
> *and from the shaking of emotions — a calm.*
> *If I were to write what today is my thought,*
> *Tomorrow it would not be —*
> *for it would blend into the silence and become me.*

As with so much of what comes "out of the mysterious depths" I knew that I did not yet understand the poem to its full extent. It contained a richness that would blossom within me 14 years later when I sought emotional growth through the practice of mindfulness meditation.

> ✥ *If I were to write a journal, an amulet to*
> *leave for future generations, hidden under my*
> *mattress or sewn within the sleeve of a coat, I*
> *would leave these words:*
> *"Ask, and it shall be given you;*
> *Seek, and you shall find;*
> *Knock and the door shall be opened unto you:*
> *For everyone that asks, receives;*
> *And he that seeks, finds; And to him that knocks,*
> *it shall be opened."*
> *But... that has already been said, hasn't it?*

Humor in the Closet

In our seminary apartment was a large hallway closet where we kept coats, clothes and stored items. One day I came home from classes, unaware that Youngman was there because the door was still locked. I entered and was walking by the hall closet towards the kitchen. Suddenly the door flew open and Youngman popped out totally naked, throwing an inner tube at me. I was shocked and then doubled up on the floor laughing until I had a belly ache. Good one.

A few weeks later, it was my turn. Hearing him coming up the stairs, I locked the door and entered the closet with the inner tube at the ready. He knocked, which I thought was odd, tried the door and finding it locked opened it with his key. Once inside he called out "Maintenance man!" Suddenly I realized that it wasn't him after all. My God! It was the maintenance guy. That's why he had knocked!

Luckily, I had not gotten naked to do the joke. I came out of the closet and said hello. The maintenance man was surprised. "Didn't you hear my knock?" He must have thought I was stupid or at least a little weird, standing there holding the innertube. I tried to explain what I was doing and how I thought he was my husband. No doubt the maintenance department had a good time with that one.

 Humor has the disassociating effect of loosening the stronghold of the ego.

Ungrounded Faith

One summer during seminary I served as a campground chaplain, where I was responsible for the outdoor worship service. After one service, a woman came up to me and said, "I wanted to tell you how much I enjoyed your sermon this morning, but I need to say something out of love. I don't think women should be ministers."

I was surprised and wondered if that 'advice' came out of love. I had an intuitive awareness that she spoke out of an anger she felt because she really wanted to be a minister, but her religious beliefs did not allow it. It seemed important to not take this personally and help her see how her beliefs affect her. "Well, that's fine," I replied. "Then, I guess being a minister is not an option for you."

One other Sunday, I was approached by a young couple who had just been to a seminar with an evangelical minister. Wild enthusiasm rang in their voices, "He said that with faith we can walk through flying bullets and not get hurt. And he told us of how this happened to missionaries in warring third world countries." They were eager to go and prove their elated faith in an area of conflict. They wanted to know if I had that kind of faith.

This was the first time I had encountered such an ungrounded, irrational type of faith. All I could think to say was,

> *"The love Jesus taught us is a love that would die for us.*
>
> *You are all excited about outlandish miracles like avoiding bullets, but I want to know, do you love me enough to die for me, because that's what Jesus did."*

Later, I found myself questioning my relationship with God. Was there something to what these kids were saying? Was I mistaken and their way is what faith is all about? I went by the lake, sat on a rock and asked God about this. Then looking down into the water to my right, a stone caught my eye. Picking it up, I discovered that it was a beautiful fossil. I knew that it took millions of years to form. It felt grounding, stable and very mysterious. It was as if God was saying, "I have always been and will always be."

> *"Faith is not a fleeting feeling of elation but an experience of eternal love lived in each concrete moment we are alive on this earth.*

It is hard to describe, but then and there it felt as if I was in the presence of eternal love. Then the thought came to me, "this rock is a sign of my covenant with you." I wrote those words on the back of the rock and have kept it to this day. And, I have never lost a sense of wonder and awe for fossils that touch us with a sense of the eternal present in a very earthy way.

Months later, I happened to catch that evangelical minister on television. The ungrounded energy of this wiry man, who appeared to have a lot of unresolved inner pain, was not unlike flying bullets. He never stopped moving and lashed out in anger at the world, while supposedly preaching the gospel of love.

Hospital Chaplaincy—Death and Rape

My next chaplaincy experience was at a large inner city hospital. The chaplaincy staff was to be called to the hospital any time there was a rape or battery. Our job was to accompany the woman through the difficult process of tests, police reports and psychiatrist visit, at her own pace, with the intent of empowering her in the process. It was an honor to be asked by the woman to stay and hold her during the difficult physical exam. I realized that I could not undo what had been done to her but I could empower her to choose how to be with it now. And I could be a sister and friend in the recovery process.

One evening a woman came into the ER after being raped. After the physical exam and the police questions, we waited for the psychiatrist intern to show up. The woman was accompanied by her twelve-year-old son and I remember being concerned for him. Together we explained what had happened, how his mother might be feeling after the rape and how much she needed him now, and how he was not to blame for what had happened.

Then the psychiatrist walked in, obviously a student and very uncomfortable with having to interview the woman. His glasses hanging off the end of his nose, he asked her questions out of the book, "Do you think you might kill yourself?" And so on. If the situation weren't so tragic, it would have been comical. I remember exchanging glances and raised eyebrows with the woman. At least she had a sense of humor. I had a new sense of what it is like to be raped and then victimized again by the system.

Once I was called to the bedside of a grieving mother and her boyfriend. I asked if they had time to be with the dead baby.

"No," she said, "he was taken away immediately, before we had a chance to even see him."

I thought that was odd and offered, "Would you like me to find him and bring him up for you to hold?"

Surprise and delight lit up their faces. "Oh, could you—please?"

I headed down to the cooler and found the fetus wrapped in paper. I brought him up to the nurses who helped me take him out of the paper and carefully place him into a newborn's blanket. With that, I went back into the parents' room and presented their child to them.

The mother held her fetus as tenderly and proudly as any mother would hold a live baby. Tears streamed down all our faces as we looked at the tiny human being, admiring his delicate fingers and toes. They were beautiful and perfect. Then the parents offered to share with me the name they had chosen for their son. This was a very sacred moment. I felt honored to be a part of their grief and recovery process.

I recall sharing this with the chaplaincy group and receiving a response of disgust from a Catholic priest, "I would never do that." All I could think was, "It's your loss."

> *Being present to others requires us to move out of our heads and into our hearts, where our own vulnerability rests.*

An Odd Dream

While I was in seminary I had a dream which stood out and in many ways noted my relationship with the church.

I was in what appeared to be a Catholic church, sitting alone, watching a group of nuns, some of whom were helping to prepare for a worship service. Priests were bustling around the altar.

As I sat there I became aware that a veil of white light had come over my head. I felt very blessed and graced. Sitting with this veil on, I realized that this was not visible to the nuns or to the priests. Then a middle aged woman sat down next to me asking if I might be able to help her with her mother. I agreed to help her, then woke up.

It never occurred to me then that my "spirituality" might not be recognized or validated by the church authorities or that my gifts might best be used in simple everyday service, especially with women. The truth of this message was not to surface until 10 years later.

> ℘ঽ *Our soul is revealed in dreams*
> *which bring to our remembrance clues to who we*
> *are*
> *and how we function in the world.*

The Stoning of Stephen

One summer my husband and I worked at a week long camp for Korean kids. I was teaching Bible classes, and some college students were helping out.

My goal was to encourage the children in finding their own relationship with God, rather than telling them how to think or feel 'spiritual'. So I made an open invitation to anyone interested, to learn how to meditate.

I began by talking about breathing and visualizing the life energy flow with each breath. The kids seemed very interested and willing to try until some resistance and fear was expressed by the college students. Later that evening my husband and I were asked to join them in a meeting. I thought nothing of it until they began to question me.

"You are teaching the children to meditate. Don't you know that meditation is not a Christian practice? What exactly are you trying to accomplish here?"

I couldn't believe what I was hearing. I remember looking at those sitting around the long table, leaning forward, accusations in their eyes. Then an intensity welled up inside of me as I leaned forward and said,

"I don't care what you guys believe, but don't ever tell me that there is something wrong about sitting in silence with God." Then we left.

As we were walking outside I had what I was later to understand as an archetypal experience. The feeling of Stephen (who was stone by a crowd) came over me. Then I became aware of what I can only describe as the heavens opening and being in the company of angels. I felt reassured on a spiritual level. My doubt and self accusations for sharing something so sacred to me and wishing I had known better were gone. The funny thing is that the stoning of Stephen was never a passage I paid much attention to.

The Truth Beneath the Anger

> Anger is only a reactive feeling;
> it is a hint of a hurt lying deep beneath the sur-
> face, waiting and wanting to be resolved.

I should have had a clue one Sunday morning before the beginning of worship that the organist at this temporary job was not going to be my best friend.

It was Sunday morning and I had brought some lupines and wild flowers for the sanctuary. I was excited about being invited to fill in for a pastor who was ill and could not fulfill his duties. As I was placing the flowers in a vase on the chancel table, the organist approached me with, "Are you doing that? We have a committee that does that." "Well," I said, "as soon as they do it, fine. I was not told that there was a committee and we have gone two Sundays without flowers. So I thought I'd bring some in."

Another Sunday she let me know that she objected to my making the sign of the cross at the benediction saying, "I didn't know Presbyterians do that. Why do you?"

One time a young woman attending worship had offered to play the piano as a special offering. Her music was very improvisational and flowed from her heart, touching me deeply. After the service I noted to the organist who was packing up to leave, that I liked the young woman's offering. "It's trash," she said flatly. "It takes a great composer and performer to do a decent improvisation. This girl is neither; all she did was goof around."

I couldn't believe my ears. "I agree that the great composers are good in a different way," I said, "but her music comes from a deep place within herself, from her relationship with God. I do not call such expressions trash."

My journal notes say that the organist kept "bitching" so I left, which was my typical way of dealing with conflict. I cannot recall a nice word from her. She would rush in to play and rush out after. We never had a chance to sit down and get to know each other.

The biggest shocker came one Sunday morning, just a few minutes before worship was to start. The organist approached me in the lounge where I was visiting with the secretary and two other women. "What time do you have?" We all gave her the time. "Fine. I will play for ten minutes then I will stop and there will be silence," she said. "All right," I replied.

Organist: "You have to start worship at nine thirty. I won't play past nine thirty. I won't fiddle around on the organ."

Me: "O.k., we can deal with the silence. When everyone is seated we will begin."

Organist: "Don't wait for them. Start at nine thirty sharp."

Me: "If people are walking in I will wait for them and start as close to nine thirty as I can."

Organist: "Our regular pastor always begins at nine thirty."

Me: "I'm not 'our regular pastor'."

Organist: "If we begin twenty minutes late, I won't play."

Me: "Then I guess we will sing acapella. I'll try to begin at nine thirty." (I begin to back up as if to leave.)

Organist: "Just start at nine thirty."

Me: "Yes ma'am!" (I salute her and turn to leave.)

Organist: "I'm not going to have us begin late ..." (she is shouting).

Me: "(Her name), would you please quit bitching at me. I just can't stand your bitching!"

Organist: "You quit bitching at me, then!"

Me: "O, God!" (I walk away, she is still "bitching." It's the only way I knew to respond to that constant, fruitless harping which felt like wild dogs tearing into something or someone beating a dead horse—only I was not dead. What in God's name did she hope to accomplish?)

Secretary: "Sorry you had an altercation with (organist). But worship should start on time."

Me: "I'll do my best. I understand the need to begin on time. I'll apologize to her." (In my notes it says, "I wish I hadn't said that. I don't feel I need to apologize, just talk and listen.)

It was hard to lead worship with this crazy feeling energy going on inside of me. I resolved to be with this later on. After worship I went to the camp and lay down in the sun on the cement slab. But even here I did not have peace. Avoidance was not the way. So I went over the incident and wrote out the dialogue in my journal. No use; peace still didn't come.

Finally, even though I dreaded the possibility of more conflicts with her, I decided to call her and make an appointment to listen to what was beneath all her anger. We met over coffee. She began in the vein of the previous argument until I explained that I needed to understand what was happening for her. Suddenly she realized I wasn't going to argue with her. Then her answer came, simple and honest:

"My concern over the starting time of worship is because I am uncomfortable improvising on the organ. It's very stressful for me. If you would just commit to starting on time, I could relax and not worry about having to improvise on the spot."

Immediately my trepidation vanished. It was good to find out the truth! Understanding where she was coming from, I promised to do my best to start on time. I also told her that I appreciated her honesty for expressing her vulnerability. After this conversation there were no more incidents.

> *Conflict offers a challenge to grow, to respond differently, and get to the essence of a problem.*

Needless to say, I felt extremely blessed when I received my first call as pastor and the organist at the church was one of the most loving, helpful, flexible, knowledgeable, creative and dearest person I could ever ask to work with. The same goes for the members of the church who often brought flowers when their gardens were blooming. It was as if the love and openness of their hearts began worship long before the official starting time.

This is not to say that there was not conflict here as well. But I felt that our firm foundation of love and mutual respect would see us all beyond any differences.

Conflict exists in every church and human association. We are often shocked that an institution based upon the love of God could have so much conflict. Perhaps the greatest lesson I learned during these years is that the only way to truly resolve conflict is by letting go of judgments, fears, and victimization.

> *The greatest gift of the church is that, with love at it's core, it has the option to return to that spirit of love which casts out all fear. When fear is gone, judgments leave and there is no need for blaming or avoidance.*

Once fear is removed, possibilities open up to see a conflict objectively, identify unmet needs, and discover the possibility for fulfillment.

> *When we acknowledge and accept our differences some common ground can be found which is often as simple as a need for mutual respect, appreciation and, of course, love.*

Chapter 7

Pastoral Experience

My First Call as Pastor

> ❦ *When we feel that we have space to truly be who we are, love and healing flow through us.*

I never lost faith that, if I surrender to God, as in meditation, God will lead me in the ongoing process of awakening or enlightenment. Since I chose to look for a solo pastorate it took me a year after graduation from seminary to find a church. This was fine with me because my goal was to work alone with a congregation so that I could hear and trust my soul. I wanted to discover what effect my leadership might have on a people of God. I didn't want to spend my time fighting an overriding male authority. Instead of fighting, I wanted to flow. And flow it did.

There were so many blissful moments as pastor. Some of the joy came in having a place in the wider community, but most of it came because I felt freed up to serve, to love and to be useful. There was something awesome about helping to provide a sacred space in the community. It was as if I was finally living outwardly what I had been for so long inwardly.

Memories of Pete

My first meeting with the pastoral search committee from the church introduced me to an elderly man named Pete. He told a story about his great grand dad, who would chew tobacco on the old wood pile, tobacco juice dripping from his mouth and down his beard, making it a strange green color. Later I always teased Pete, that it was this story that helped me decide to accept the call to pastor the church. I figured that if the people loved stories and had a sense of humor, if they were anything like Pete, I'd like living there.

Much of the work in the church was accomplished by the farmers and retired men who were such a delight. With every project I heard stories about the church past and the community that informed me and gave me a much deeper appreciation of the people I was serving.

It was my first Sunday at the church. I had no idea that my retired friend Pete in the middle pew was taking his usual mid sermon nap. During the sermon, I was recounting what I had overheard on a recent airplane trip. The man on the plane had been repeatedly swearing in the name of the Lord. I leaned towards the microphone and repeated his words, "Jesus, Christ!" in a booming tone to make it clear that he was not praying, but swearing. Pete jumped two feet out of his pew and awoke to congregational chuckles. At the check-out line after worship he told me what had happened and swore that he would never again sleep during the sermon.

Perhaps the greatest compliment a pastor can be paid is to be told, "I would like you to be the one officiating at my funeral". Sometimes there are so many other pastoral needs to take care of that we don't really take time to appreciate such a request. But that did not happen with Pete. "Will you do my funeral?" he once asked me after a funeral service. I told him, "Of course I will; it would be an honor."

Months later, as he lay in his hospital bed dying of cancer he reminded me of my promise. "I'm not doing your funeral!" I said teasing him, "I want you to recover and keep on giving us all a hard time." But he knew better than I did. He died a week later. His was one of the hardest funerals I have officiated at, only to be topped by the funeral of my father. Even now, five years later, I find tears in my eyes as I recall the humor, love and feisty nature of my retired friend, Pete.

 ... a time to weep and a time to laugh; a time to mourn and a time time to dance ...

Ecc. 3:4

Buggers in My Pocket

One of the greatest joys of serving the church is being with the children. I often delighted in sitting with them for a few minutes in the pew before service, and playing with them afterward.

One day an adorable little girl, Jamie, came up to me in the check out line after worship and with her mother standing nearby, proudly announced: "I have buggers in my pocket!" Her innocently bold and playful words were delightfully disassociating for me and I sensed the sacredness of our conversation.

 I will always love the way children bring what we judge as profane into the realm of the sacred. What a wonderful gift to experience the world through the open eyes and heart of a child.

So I looked in the pocket she was so proudly holding out, but saw nothing. Then, with the best imitation I could muster, I announced to her, "I have buggers in my pocket too and mine are bigger than yours because I have a bigger nose!" She looked at me quizzically for a moment, as if to make sense of this strange reply. Then she declared: "My Daddy must have really big buggers because his nose is so big!"

The following week Jamie's mother scolded me in mock anger, "Reverend Julie, ever since last Sunday, when you encouraged her, Jamie has been telling everyone she meets that she has buggers in her pocket and her entire conversations have revolved around buggers! It's been so embarrassing. She has even been going up to strangers in the grocery store and announcing with great pride and delight that she has buggers in her pocket. Thanks a lot!"

How Do You Know There Is a God?

The headiness of our denomination may be changing slowly. The difference between my generation and the pastors before me was vividly illustrated at a meeting of my fellow clergy. I had arrived late and an informal discussion was already in process. When I entered the lead pastor pointed at me and laughed saying "There is a good example!" I joined in by asking what's so funny and was asked, "How do you know there is a God?" To which I replied "I experience God." To which he replied "Exactly! In my day you knew there was a God because you understood God intellectually. In your generation you know God from experience."

Perhaps when our denomination begins to be less afraid of experience it will see that everything is of God and nothing is outside of God. Then, it will be okay to share our experiences of the holy without being labeled as weird or flaky. Hopefully then too, the practice of spiritual direction which focuses on the human experience of God, will be given more validation.

Friday, Sunday and the Firemen

Sometimes loving a people means asking
if what we are doing on Friday
is consistent with our worship on Sunday.

I did that the Sunday after the firemen's festival. For my sermon, I had prepared the statistics of drunk driving, fairground brawls the local police were involved with, and a death suit from the family of a woman who left the fair one year and was killed on the highway from drunk driving. With this, I went up to the pulpit.

I recounted a story the chief of police told me about a farmer from another community who came to our fair just to get away for a while and while visiting our fair, was attacked by a drunken man.

I repeated word for word the stories of members of our community seeing people defecate in their flower beds and copulate on their lawn. "Did you say something to them?" I had asked the young man who saw the couple prone in his yard. "No," he replied laughing. "They were in a bed of fire ants and I figured that was enough punishment!"

I asked if there was not some irony that the very folks who put on the fair and sell (indeed often pushed) the beer, were the same ones who had to extricate the woman from her car with the jaws of life.

I then asked the congregation if having the biggest beer tent in the county was worth all this, and whether we really wanted to be known in this way.

I suppose there would have been no problem if some of the more influential members of the volunteer fire department didn't just happen to also be members of our congregation. Or if we didn't happen to have the Zor Shriners visiting with us that day. An older member of the congregation noted that it was a sermon we needed to hear but that I should not have given it when we had guests — i.e. don't air our dirty laundry. Actually, a member of the Shriners who sang for us that day told me it was a great sermon and I had a lot of guts.

I didn't realize just how much guts it would take to live with the sermon once it was preached. Later that week I met with two other clergy from the community who said, "We heard about your sermon, congratulations we're behind you." I asked them "How far behind me are you?" They laughed and said "Far."

Little did I know that I had taken on the "old boy network" of our growing community. It had been reported to me that after the sermon, some of the firemen were talking about "calling you down to the fire station."

The following year I spoke with the festival coordinator to see if we could put up a table to paint faces for free. I was basically told by the man that I had been a bad girl last year because of the sermon I preached. I asked him, "Have you actually read the sermon?" (I always have copies available and I knew one had been taken to the fire station.) "No, I haven't read it," he replied, "but you should know that we can make things hard for you around here."

"Are you threatening me?" I asked and added, "I'm not afraid of your old boy network. This community is growing and you don't hold the power you used to anymore."

> For me, the inner message and life has to be consistent with the outer message and life. I like that. I call it integrity.

I can't say that this didn't color my work at the church. I spent lots of time in inner examination. Did I do something "wrong?" Why was this inner/outer thing so important that I would jeopardize my job? Something was bothering me, but I was not in touch with the source of it yet.

I realized that I was changing and growing in ways the church could not grow. No longer was there room in my life for unexamined psychological clutter. How can we be where we are if it is only superficial? Can we welcome new people on Sunday and then, inadvertently, slap them in the face on Monday with words or actions that stem from the unexamined gooey mess inside of us? This gave me all the more desire to move on to a place where I could grow and examine and release all my goo so that inner and outer would match.

My own unexamined psychological clutter was also surfacing. Shortly after preaching the fireman's sermon I had a dream which disturbed me and indicated that I had some stuff I needed to look into as well. In the dream I was going for a lovely walk on a wide path in the woods. Occasionally, I bent over to admire the foliage. As I bent over I became aware that I had started a fire. I was startled to discover that the fire was started by a lit torch I was carrying. I felt very bad about starting the fire and, ironically, the firemen had to come and put it out! I didn't know how to be with this dream at the time. It was easy to see that it triggered some discomfort and guilt.

Years later, when I returned to do a baptism at the church I was told that, while searching for a new minister, one fireman was reported to have said, "I don't want any more fiery redheaded ministers in the pulpit!"

Facing the Dragon

> "In myths the hero is the one who conquers
>
> the dragon, not the one who is devoured by it....
> Also, he is no hero who never met the dragon,
> or who, if he once saw it,
> declared afterwards that he saw nothing....
> Only one who has risked the fight with the drag-
> on
> and is not overcome by it
> wins the hoard, the 'treasure hard to obtain.'"
>
> Carl Jung

I had a thirst to understand what was happening both inside myself and in others. After reading *Dreams and Healing* by John Sanford, I made an entry in my journal.: "I recall as I read this, a dream I had as a child. In the dream I was in Ford Field Park being chased by a bear when I suddenly turned and said to the bear, "Lets be friends," and at once we skipped down the hill arm in arm. Did the bear represent my unconscious? My fears?

Ever since that dream, I have been much less afraid to engage in struggles — be they inner or outer. In fact, it may be that in my work as a preacher, I may be bringing some of the collective unconscious of the community to the surface, getting us to face our dragons — as with the Fireman's festival sermon.... It is like a cleansing. We don't necessarily solve anything but we can at least become aware of it once it reaches the light of day.

After reading much Jung and Sanford, I realize that I seem to intuit in an almost unconscious manner what people are struggling with and how to nurture/confront those things so that they can be faced and integrated into the whole person.

Healing and wholeness
do not take place
until the boil is lanced
and our worst fears are faced.

Six months later I wrote: "My spirit is restless to be about the work and things of God. The church seems stagnant - holding to the past and fearful of the future. I too have become angry and fear filled."

I sought help from a Catholic center but their spiritual director was not in so I signed up for a lecture from James Finley that Friday. I asked God to bless Friday's retreat. As my entry shows, I was ready to find the answers I sought:

"God, bring me, I beg you, into a new understanding
of your call and purpose for me and my husband.
Teach us how we might reflect your divine light
and glorify you... strengthen my compassion
and my passion for you. Destroy my arrogance
and grant me humility. Lead me."

When the Student is Ready, the Teacher Appears

At the retreat, James Finley quoted a holy man who said,

"I cannot find the place where I stop and
God begins."

Finley also said,

> "Each of us is living a constant unfolding
> death, moving from who we used to be into who
> we not yet are."

And he spoke of how we needed to have courage in the face of radical transformation. Then he shared an analogy which I shared with my congregation on Sunday and would share with many others:

> "Before wood is transformed into fire
> it crackles and makes lots of noise.
> Then the wood becomes all fire and is quiet.
> Wood is our self/ego and the fire is God."

This would come back to me years later when I was going through the fires of mid-life and burned this rendition of an old Sufi saying into the mantle of our house:

> "Love is the essence of my being.
> Love is fire and I am wood burnt by the flame.
> Let love move in and adorn this house
> until myself ties up its bundle and leaves
> and what remains is God."
>
> My rendition of a Sufi Saying

The other reason this was such a wonderful retreat was the time it gave me to sort through what was happening inside me and in my role as a minister. It was a seemingly dark period and I felt as if I was wrapped in a shroud of darkness and mystery. When the talks gave way to a break I would remain on the floor in the back and meditate. I had tried to sit in the chairs but was not comfortable. People were enjoying his words and chuckling at the truth in them.

I was not in a mood to chuckle. They were in an auditorium; I was in a spiritual ER.

This was clearly a deeply introspective period. In recalling this time, I noted that the feeling and depth it demanded had an intensity not unlike my mid-life energy some three years later.

Honoring My Need to Explore the Unconscious

 Times of change and transition are often difficult.
It would be easier to stay as we are,
but something inside calls out to
"...Come, explore the mystery, do not be afraid."

Our personal, unresolved issues always affect our behavior and ability to act out of love. One frustration I had with the church is that we teach and preach love but it cannot be lived out unless those personal things which block it are acknowledged and resolved. It was frustrating for me because I sensed these personal blocks but did not have the training to explore or resolve them, although I did at various points try.

The truth is that we all bring to every event and meeting our own personal issues.
When we are not conscious of these, they tend to lend a particular flavor to the event,
which really has nothing to do with the topic at hand.

The best thing to do, it seemed, was to get the training I needed to do my own inner work and to facilitate it in others.

Since what's going on deep inside of us—at the unconscious level—is at the heart of how we act and respond, what we value and our ability to love, it made sense to focus upon that.

Leaving My Faith Family

It was not easy to leave a people whom I had grown close to and come to love and respect. In the end, it would take a full three years before I could think of my church family without an aching loss. I felt tremendous gratitude for having had the opportunity to pastor this small church and to become involved in the lives of such wonderful people. I had learned some good lesson here, given and received a lot and grown in ways that now called for me to move on.

It was hard to leave but I knew that leaving was the best option. I had a need to grow and I couldn't ask the church to be where I needed to be. I needed to honor where they were and seek my own growth needs myself.

Chapter 8

EMBODIED SPIRITUALITY

Connecting With My Body

I was accepted into the Spiritual Direction internship at Mercy Center in California. Here I had time to just be. Time to reflect, take stock, focus and grow. Any 'doing' that was taking place was done mindfully, in the context of 'being'. A nice thing about being in "school" for me is that it provides the space to "do" nothing without feeling guilty.

I loved walking to a local coffee house, finding a space there to sit and make notes for wood burning ideas or work on this text. I had a sense of "present and impending growth" as if all is well. This was one of the first times since the days of the camp where I really just allowed myself to be without overriding outer obligations. This is reflected in a poem I wrote while in the coffee house:

> *Spirit guiding, senses aligning,*
> *time to breathe and be.*
> *I sit in the shadow with a heart that is fallow,*
> *attending the Mystery.*

During this time I became aware that though I was not at the camp, aspects of the sacred ground of the camp were here too, for I was learning more and more that the sacredness of the camp was a metaphor for my soul:

> ♨ *Hollyhocks, purple cone flowers,*
> *cement embankments,*
> *crooked broken sidewalks and thimble berries.*
> *What do the camp and Marin County*
> *have in common?*
> *Hills, pine trees, water, fresh air and deer*
> *make it the same there as here.*

The program at Mercy Center was run by the Catholic Sisters of Mercy and it was excellent.

I realized I would learn a lot when my supervisor asked me "What are you feeling right now?" and I replied, "I don't know." It surprised me that I didn't know what I was feeling because I am such a feeling person.

Years later as I was helping others to become aware of their feelings just as my supervisor helped me, I began to notice a pattern. 'Intuitive feelers' (The intuitive feeler personality type along with others is described in *Please Understand Me: Character and Temperament Types*, by David Keirsey & Marilyn Bates) are very aware of what others are feeling but unaware of what they themselves feel. Not being in touch with one's own feeling is a survival mechanism of this personality type. Our heightened sensitivity to significant others affects us deeply. As a result we are often acting according to what we perceive to be the other's feelings, but not being true to our own feelings. If someone is sad we become the clown, if they are angry we soothe them and so on. Our cues come from outside of us. That is why we are such good nurses, pastors and caretakers in general.

But there are two basic difficulties with this survival mechanism. First of all, we lose ourselves and get out of touch with our own feelings. Second, we intuit what others feel and then assume the cause of their feelings. Our intuition is usually correct but our assumptions are not; they just come from our own "stuff". So, as intuitive feelers, we need to learn two things — first what we ourselves are feeling, and second, how to check things out with others.

These lessons are easier to learn when we realize that people need to be exactly where they are, feeling exactly what they are feeling. Connected to that realization is the fact that our desire to make everyone happy and move them into a space different from where they are is really just our own need for comfort. This is a major learning process for intuitive feelers.

> *When we become aware of and comfortable with our own feelings, we won't feel the need to move others out of theirs.*

The Spiritual Direction Internship taught me some important lessons about inner wellness:

> *Wellness cannot be reached by moving away from our feelings or moving others away from theirs. True wellness comes from freely feeling what is there for us. True compassionate companionship comes from allowing others to be just as they are.*
> *Then love is manifested and healing takes place.*

> *Those in our environment reflect ourselves back to us — one way or another.*

Without these insights, I could never have been a spiritual director or developed the art of Inner Listening.

At the Internship, I also became aware of the connection between identifying my feelings and maintaining present moment awareness.

> Future orientation keeps me out of the present moment and unaware of my feelings. How can we be 'here' if we are already 'out there'? And how can we get 'there' if we are not 'here' first? Both past and future orientations are ways to avoid the present feeling moment.

Mary and Elizabeth

A young woman, we'll call her Jenny, came to a session complaining that she had images of bearing a child. She mentioned that all her life, she had sought and affirmation of self-worth outside herself. I remember asking, "And where do you think you will really find life?" She replied, "Inside myself."

It was then that I realized that her 'problem' of imaging a child within herself was really not a problem, but a symbol of the gift of a new beginning for her. She too saw that. Then, without warning, I had an archetypal experience of Mary and Elizabeth which seemed to "come down" over me. It was as if I was Elizabeth, already pregnant by the spirit, and visited by my cousin Mary. Mary had just been visited by the angel and wanted to talk about the spirit growing inside herself. Who did she go to? Of course to someone who had a similar experience. I felt so honored and humbled that this young Mary of the 21st Century should come to me.

Later, an older woman on retreat who I was directing shared this story with me: "Last night I happened to come upon the icon of Mary and Elizabeth, and I thought of us."

Since then, I have held Mary and Elizabeth as an archetype for spiritual direction.

Learning to Look Below the Surface

Once during an internship session, a young man was sharing various ideas with me. The trouble was that he went on and on, boring me almost to tears. To be polite and show I was listening, I asked superficial questions, which had the effect of keeping the conversation on a heady level.

When I reported the session to my supervisor, he asked me, "What was happening that you kept asking more questions?" I said, "I was trying to act polite and interested." He then asked, "Why did you need to make such an effort?" I said, "Because I was bor... " I stopped myself. "You were what?" he asked. "I was bored" I said with embarrassment.

My supervisor smiled. "What would you have done if you acknowledged your boredom instead of judging it?" Amazed by his question and feeling the grace of it, I said, "I would have changed the conversation, gotten him out of his head, and into what he had really come to spiritual direction for." My supervisor smiled again and we shared a quiet sacred moment as I realized how judgment of my boredom kept me from acknowledging it and using it to help the situation.

Now I help clients get at what it is they are seeking very early on, because to do less would dishonor the intention of their soul and the whole purpose of their visit. The effect of this experience still gives me courage to help a client get to the heart of the matter. And, oh yeah, I don't care to be bored!

Jim, another directee, would walk around and around in circles, driving me nuts and making it difficult for me to help him let go and just be with what was happening. Then one night I saw Jim and myself in a dream. He was on one side of a chain link fence, I was on the other looking at him. Suddenly his head went up in flames. I woke up. "Wow!" I said, "Is he angry!" Then, remembering that my environment reflects myself back to me, I asked with hesitancy, "Am I angry?" Suddenly, my belly extended beyond anything I ever felt, and of it's own accord, took in a deep breath of air. I lay in bed breathing for a while, then I got up to take notes: "There is a feeling I needed to be with."

> 🌱 *There is nothing I recognize on the outside*
> *which is not already on the inside.*

A Model to Embody Experience

Inspired by the wisdom and grace of Ken Wilber's marvelous work, *No Boundary,* and my experiences at Mercy Center, I created my integration model for spiritual direction.

The model was based upon a reoccurring dream I had as a child. I was at the top of a circular staircase, like the ones in State Capital buildings. In the dream, I would jump into the center of the spiral. It seemed nothing for me to jump from one level to another or dive into the dark abyss below. So, my model for spiritual growth became a spiral.

> ✿ *In order to evolve spiritually*
> *we sometime have to take a leap of faith*
> *and jump into those places which seem dark,*
> *knowing that the darkness is not dark to God*
> *and that at the base is the un-nameable mystery,*
> *the source of life.*

According to this model, spiritual growth indicates releasing into the mystery which is already inside ourselves. I prefer this model to the more common notion to "climb the ladder" of spirituality, which puts us ahead or behind others, seems egocentric and leaves little room for mystery.

Spiral Model for spiritual direction

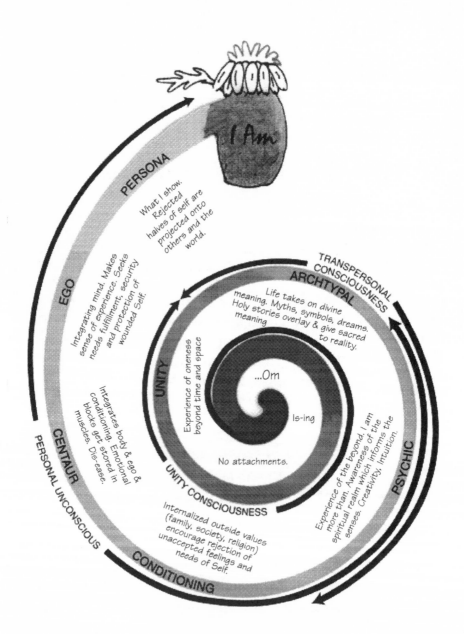

PERSONA — What I show. Rejected halves of self are projected onto others and the world.

EGO — Integrating mind. Makes sense of experience. Seeks fulfillment, security needs and protection of wounded Self.

CENTAUR — Integrates body & ego & conditioning. Emotional blocks get stored in muscles. Dis-ease.

PERSONAL UNCONSCIOUS

CONDITIONING — Internalized outside values (family, society, religion) encourage rejection of unaccepted feelings and needs of Self.

PSYCHIC — Experience of the beyond. I am more than. Awareness of the spiritual realm which informs the senses. Creativity. Intuition.

TRANSPERSONAL CONSCIOUSNESS

ARCHTYPAL — Life takes on divine meaning. Myths, symbols, dreams. Holy stories overlay & give sacred meaning to reality.

UNITY — Experience of oneness beyond time and space

UNITY CONSCIOUSNESS

...Om

Is-ing

No attachments.

I Am

Description of the Model for Inner Listening

Over the years, since the internship, I have distilled spiritual direction into its most fundamental element—Inner Listening.

> *Inner Listening is based upon simply being present, without judgment, to what already is. As we go inside of ourselves, we come face to face with all the aspects of 'I AM'.*

I have found that the values and norms of acceptable behavior which we learn as children (conditioning) determine which aspects of ourselves we later bring out and develop, and which other aspects we deem unacceptable and repress. When the conflict between different aspects of ourselves becomes intolerable, we might rebel and unleash our anger or show only those acceptable, pleasing aspects of ourselves (persona).

In Inner Listening, we access the wounded Self by starting at the centaur level and quietly staying present to the bodily felt energy blocks. This uncovers the defense and protection mechanisms of the ego, often experienced as inner images or feelings. By simply witnessing these defenses, we allow them to unfold into other images, feelings and memories which reveal the wounded parts of Self and its unmet needs.

Listening to those unmet needs allows emotional release, which leads to a release of bodily energy. This is often felt as heat and "a huge weight being lifted off." We are now in communion with the essence of the Self, where we experience peace, calm, love, glowing energy, relaxation, a connected body and a sense of being "more than"—an experience which leads into transpersonal consciousness or unity consciousness and Is-ing.

Breath, Releasement and Receiving

One morning as I was walking the dogs along a mountain trail, it occurred to me that I often thought of inhaling as receiving spirit, but hadn't placed much attention on exhaling. What if the release and emptying during the out-breath was the best way for me to imagine the spirit entering?

It took a little practice to retrain my inner imagining. I realized that when I received upon inhaling, I was making an effort to receive. When I breathed out, however, spirit simply filled the places which had just been emptied.

> ❋ *When receiving spirit upon each exhalation,*
> *there is a sense, not of work and effort but of*
> *grace*
> *and an opening to what already is.*

Then I began a dance of the breath, noticing what was already happening and flowing with it. Receiving from the earth, through my feet, releasing to the spirit entering through the top of my head.

Years later I would use this exercise with clients whose energy was spinning and needed to be centered and grounded. I have them imagine the life force of the earth coming into their feet or through the base of their 1st chakra or energy center (at the base of the spine) as the color red. The energy they are releasing into the top of the head is imagined to be as the color of the 7th chakra, white. These naturally seem to mix at the heart chakra, often depicted as pink.

In my work, this intentional breathing technique helps to open and heal the heart center while grounding and centering the client. Not only does it have a calming effect, but it brings them into a deeper state of being, where they are more embodied and ready to begin inner exploration.

Passing On the Light

One weekend, my new friend Steve, a chiropractor in San Anselmo, CA. was having a Jin Shin Do workshop. Jin Shin Do is a body-mind acupressure treatment developed by Iona Teegarden. The combination of acupressure and helping the client verbalize their feelings helps release stored energy and memories from the body and mind.

When the practice time came, I worked on my partner first, then she worked on me. Steve and Iona walked in and out supervising us. Midway through, Steve began assisting my partner, and as my chiropractor, he knew some non-acupressure points where I was holding energy in the form of arthritis. Just then Iona walked in and seeing where Steve was holding said, "That's not a pressure point, Steve." To which he replied, "I know, but it is one of hers."

Pressing these points began to change things. First I noted that everyone else seemed to be done and we really didn't have time for this. My resistance was shot down when they both said, "We will be here for you for however long it takes." I wasn't used to having people serve me. It felt odd. But their caring and non-judgmental way of being with me helped me relax into the session. What happened next was a complete surprise.

I told Steve, "I feel a lot of uncomfortable energy." Steve asked me "Where do you feel it?" I pointed to my upper chest and he put a hand on the spot making it possible for me to be with it. Soon after my hands curled up, my legs drew in and I felt very tiny. Then I turned onto my side and rolled up into a ball. "Don't leave me alone," I said then I cried for a moment and rested. When it was over, I remember standing up and feeling for the first time as if my energy was totally free flowing. The arthritis in my right hip that had made walking to the workshop a painful experience was totally gone. Totally.

> ɝ❧ *For healing to take place, it is not the particular technique that counts. What counts is being unconditionally present to the other.*

From this experience I learned that it is best to listen to the unique messages of the body to determine how and where our touch will help release blocked energy.

That evening was strange. I hardly slept as I had lots of energy. Yet it was not restlessness, but good feeling energy. Then I noticed something odd. I could still feel Steve's hand on my upper chest. In the morning, as I was walking the dogs in the beautiful hills, I conversed in prayer asking God, "Why do I still feel Steve's hand there?" The answer was clear, "It is not Steve's hand, but my own."

The next day in the spiritual direction internship I was very much in the present moment, very peaceful and centered and aware of what was happening on an energy level both in myself and in others. The following afternoon I had a female directee who longed to be held by the Goddess. I asked, "Do you feel this longing in your body?" She pointed to her chest. I became aware of a very strong feminine energy coming from the left side of my body and moving out to the place she indicated.

I knew that this would be a very healing touch for her. On the other hand, I was aware that, although it had not been stated, we probably don't use touch in spiritual direction work. But the energy of light I felt running through my body was stronger than the energy of fear, and I trusted it more than the fear of going against the rules.

"If at any point you want me to place my hand there, all you need to do is place your hand there and ask me to place mine there as well" I told her. A few minutes later she did just that. I checked it out again with her. Then pulling my chair alongside hers, I placed my left hand on the middle of her upper chest. I knew I was taking a risk but I knew that when things happen on this subtle, intuitive level, I trust them.

As I drove to the internship the next day I knew that I was going to share this experience with the group. I had a running inner dialogue all the way there and made an effort to just breath and trust the process.

At our group meeting, I told the supervisors and internship group what I had done and why. But instead of using the good listening and discerning techniques we had been taught, the interns went around explaining whether they would or wouldn't have done what I did. Of course, I told them, I would not expect them to do what I did. Our experiences are different, and the guidance to touch came directly out of the healing energy I was experiencing from the day before. I had encountered this healing, guiding energy before, and knew it to be like a direct link to my own divine essence. I trusted it. Without this, the action would have been empty.

The confrontation was difficult for me. I was filled with fear for the rest of the day. Some of the interns assured me that if that is how God is working in my life go with it. But the fear lingered. Our group counselor noted that I seemed to have touched in a clinically correct manner. She also noted that the issue for me seemed to be one of inner versus outer authority.

When I went to bed that night, I asked God to remove the fear which had gripped me. Then I realized, "Fear hasn't gripped me, I have gripped the fear!" So instead I prayed for help in releasing it. Suddenly I felt a ping, ping, ping sensation, shooting down my legs. I realized that the fear was gone. Even thinking about the fear did not bring it back.

> ༃ *The body does not distinguish between reality and fantasy. Much if not all of our fear and tension springs from fantasies of the future or the past.*

The next session with the directee I had 'touched' came around and I asked her how she was. She said that at first she was mad because she wanted the Goddess to hold her. Then, as she walked along a beautiful tree lined street, she heard the Goddess respond.

Her answer was not unlike the one I received. "I did hold you. I hold you through others." Suddenly, she felt her chest open up and she felt free.

The next time I saw Steve, I shared this with him. He told me about a dream one woman had at the end of a week long workshop he had attended, which introduced him to Jin Shin Do.

> ᴂ *The woman dreamt that she was standing on a mountain. A light had come into her and she touched two people who were then filled with light. The two she touched then touched two more and so on until all the people on the mountain were filled with light.*

Chapter 9
MID-LIFE CRISIS

The Outer Reflects the Inner

Sitting with the real estate agent, I was on my 3rd cup of water and thinking, 'God, I have been so thirsty and shaky!' I was confronting the agent about different things while apologizing at the same time. We were just buying a house, so why was I feeling so sultry and nervous?

I reflected upon 'being nervous' for a few days. Being nervous is okay. It's the way it is at the moment. There was nothing to hide and I couldn't hide it even if I wanted to. This was strange. Something was going on and I didn't know what.

Remodeling More Than a House

My first clue that more was being remodeled than just the house, came one warm July day while I was potting and my builder and his young helper were sawing 2x6's. I was blissful. Happy to be potting and happy to have company. There was a sense of rightness and deep inner peace about the morning, and it seemed only appropriate when the builder began to share a dream he had that evening.

In his charming boyish way, he described his dream of being in a church with a female minister.

Then it was my turn.

"Well as long as we are sharing dreams, I confess that I had one about you." Somewhat embarrassed and glancing over from my pottery, I began, "I was somewhere I had never been, I was crazy, so your girlfriend told you to take me to where I belong."

The builder looked up from his 2x6 and said, "but I don't know where you belong."

"I know you don't," I replied, "and you didn't know in my dream either. So I just sat on your lap for 5 minutes, then continued on my way and I woke up."

Somewhere deep in our unconscious, I thought, we must be reflecting the anima and animus for each other—he was reflecting my masculine side and I his feminine. Perhaps his feminine was freeing and he was in the process of integrating it.

As for me, my getting where I belong and integrating my masculine was not going to happen as I sought—through outward male figures—but it would have to happen on my own which makes me feel "lost" sometimes. And although there will be people along the way with whom I can sit and find comfort, they cannot take me to where I belong because they do not know. Only I know and I had that sense in my dream, that deep inside I knew where to go, if I would just listen.

Something was drawing me to my builder. It felt good to stand close and although conversation was happening on an outer level, there seemed to be an intuitive one going on below the surface.

One damp rainy day while the guys were working on the ceilings, I lit a fire in the fireplace and reread parts of *The Call and The Echo; Sufi Dreamwork and the Psychology of the Beloved* by Llewellyn Vaughn-Lee. I was opening to my unconscious mind and present to the mystical nature of the moment. There was comfort in the rhythmic lull of the saw, just twenty feet away. The fire was good, the company was good, and the book was good. If I had died, I already would have been in Heaven.

I read a passage in the book that describes the Sufi understanding of how human love is a love for God and that even the passion of human love unconsummated, leads the mystic into union with the beloved. I had a deep sense that this was what the present moment was about. Then I found a passage in the book, which I revised, and decided to wood burn it into the mantle of the fireplace:

> "The greatest battle is to do battle with oneself.
> The greatest adventure and the most difficult task
> is to enter into the darkness of our own being
> and come face to face
> with the "Mystery" called God.
> The sword of the warrior is needed
> for this inner journey.
> Let it be a sword tempered with love
> and blessed with the wisdom of understanding
> until the ego has surrendered
> and there are no battles
> because everything belongs and is accepted."
>
> my rendition of a Sufi reaching

How appropriate these words. Not only for my own inner growth, but for the work I do as a spiritual director.

Just above the mantle I would hang pictures of the four buddhist temple guards of the north, south, east and west, which Youngman and I bought from a vendor who came to the Peace Corps office in Korea. The guards are dressed in flowing robes and holding onto swords. The swords had always held energy for me. Now they were to have center stage, representing the inner journey and a beautiful integration of male, female, earth and spirit energy.

> When the energies of the mid-life crisis are in place, this can be a powerful deepening experience—not only of our sexuality but also of our spirituality.

In the evenings I would spend hours just sitting in the unfinished doorway of our new home. One foot on the grass outside and one on the cement slab inside. This was a physical placing symbolizing my sense of soul place as this poem reflects:

> 🦢 *Let me sit right in-between,*
> *where the doorway meets the sky.*
> *Where mortals walk in grasses green*
> *and angel voices sigh.*

I Could Have Made Love to a Door

It would have been great if this was all there was to it. But the days I was not at the house were hell. I longed to be involved in the activities at the house, and would find excuses to go back. Worse yet, when I thought of my builder, my body would respond physically. My second chakra, the energy center for sexuality, was going crazy. I was like a cat in heat and could have made love to a door. I hardly ate or slept. What was going on? My chiropractor noticed that I had lost a lot of weight, so he began to ask questions as if I were anorexic. "I'm not eighteen any more, it's just the work on the house. I'm fine," I said defensively.

As I listened to myself, I wondered why eighteen had come up. Could something from twenty-two years ago still be affecting me? I hadn't felt such teenage passion since before Philippe died. Even my body was reverting to the figure I had at eighteen. Was my second chakra opening up now in the presence of my builder's energy? Had I somehow closed it down for years?

The builder was going to be done with the house within a few weeks, but I knew that I would be left unfinished. The thought of being left in this state frightened me. I needed to find out what was happening to me, so I decided to talk with him. The thought scared me. I didn't mind revealing my feelings, but I feared asking for his time.

He was late. The wait was agonizing. A stabbing pain shot through my third chakra or power center (the solar plexus), matched only by the pain I had in Korea when I was growing a huge intestinal parasite that would whip around and stop me in my tracks. With that, I realized that unless I talked with him I was going to be immobilized.

When he arrived, I asked him for forty-five minutes. He graciously agreed. We sat outside, side by side and I introduced the topic. "Do you really think talking is going to help?" he asked. I said, "It should help the energy to shift."

So, in halting phrases with long pauses, I shared the turmoil of my inner life. He listened. It was the most grace-filled, compassionate listening I had experienced in a long time, and for which I will always be grateful.

"I was aware there was something going on. You don't think the attraction is just sexual?" he asked.

"Nothing," I said, "is just sexual; it's all tied into everything else. There is probably a lot of projection going on. And, in spite of a strong sexual attraction to you, I don't want an affair. I already married the person I want to grow old with."

Then he told me a bit of his life's story. We were two strangers sitting on a hill talking of the most intimate things and yet we did not seem like strangers. That was on a Friday. We joked the rest of the day about shifting energy which hadn't shifted yet. But I kept saying, "It will!"

> *We see in others repressed qualities within ourselves which would make us whole. We get hung up on the qualities of others, not realizing that those very qualities are but reflections of qualities within ourselves which are calling out to be honored. The deeper the passion or dispassion for it on the outside, the greater the need to recognize it within.*

The Shift

It was a gorgeous sunrise, and I enjoyed watching it from a rock outside our house. This has been my place of morning worship since we no longer attend church. I took with me a chakra chart and some books by Barbara Brennan which have always been helpful. For a moment on the rock, the significance of the events within me and my builder became clear. The psychology of the second chakra activity was brought into perspective. Then I began to feel the energy shift from my second chakra upward. I was elated and energized.

This was made all the easier because he had finished his work on our home early. The place looked great. There was but one thing left to do after the roofers were done, which he would come back to do in a month.

Although it was difficult, I shared my inner struggles with my husband. For me, keeping everything above board was the healthiest and the most respectful of my life partner. Now I had inner and outer turmoil, and no support for either. I tried to make it clear to Youngman that this was my stuff I was dealing with and no one else needed to be blamed or held responsible. Not unlike Inner Listening work, my husband and I had to face some scary moments in our relationship in order to get to the place where we knew we were blessed.

Over the next couple of weeks I was intentional about feeling my 2nd chakra energy cords disconnecting from my builder. It was painful not to have him around, but, I also knew that it was not healthy for me to be connected to him. He had his own life and I had to get on with finding out where I belong.

> It is important to take back our projections that others are carrying so well for us, and to see those qualities within ourselves.

We spoke briefly when he came back to finish the job a month later. Our eyes connected during a pause in our conversation, and...

Vumph!

It felt as if a packet of energy had just shot into my eyes and down to my womb. I sat there mildly shocked, feeling like a cat in heat again.

That evening the sexual energy within me was the strongest ever. My body seemed to be literally undulating. I noted with humor that if this were a movie and someone saw me they would probably call for an exorcism. I tried to roll with the flow of energy and not judge it. Over the next few days I had a deep desire to be totally surrendered and in sexual union. This hot passion, however, was strictly mine and an affair was not going to solve my issue (I admit that I had finally suggested we "just do it" and get it over with, but he refused, thank heavens). I sought out a therapist who encouraged me to deal creatively with this new energy.

The hormonal haze was powerful and hard to shake. It would have been a blessing to share it with a supportive group that had various experiences of the mid-life crisis. I wanted to get beyond the emotional aspects to help discern the issues, patterns and growth taking place. But for now, I just had to be with the feelings.

The Biggest Rock in the Neighborhood

A male acquaintance had summed up my struggle with the phrase, "you just want to get laid." This may have been true on a surface level but did not sum up a desire for union in its deepest sense. I felt that there was more going on here than "just sex".

The next morning I woke up very early and began to make a clay sculpture of two people in sexual union. I called it "Sex is more than just getting laid." Later that day I did another piece. At the time, I felt like creating a set of pieces in stone all under the theme of unity. On my walks with the dogs I wrote a song to thank and release our builder from carrying my projections. From now on, if it was guy stuff I needed in my life, I would have to do it for myself.

I called a quarry upstate and arranged to fly out there with my father and pick out an enormous stone for a sculpture. The rocks there were massive and the tires on the quarry trucks seemed as big as houses. An excavator said that he could move a rock weighing no more than 5 tons, so I selected a 5-tonner.

I asked my sister to accompany me to the local hardware store. In the aisle of the tool belts and chisels I began modeling and hamming it up for my sister. We were in stitches. I picked out a perfect little tool belt. Later on that week, I went to an outlet for a pair of jeans since the ones I had were falling off. I tried on size seven but they hung as well. The young man helping suggested I needed a size six. I was shocked that I had lost so much weight. I chose a nice pair of "guy boots," researched air compressors and pneumatic tools and when the stone arrived was ready to begin.

The sculpture was to be a sitting meditative figure, hands in an open prayer at the heart. I called it "Namaste." It would sit in an outside cove of the house or by the pond, welcoming the world with the phrase, "the divine in me acknowledges the divine in you." I figured that by the time it was finished I would have chiseled away tons of stone and, hopefully gotten rid of as much excess in me as well. The sculpture is yet to be completed.

When the rock arrived in mid October, the excavator had only a front end loader to move it, as his larger equipment was on another job. "No problem, I can move a 5-ton-baby with that front loader," he said.

Two hours later, he called me over. White limestone powder covered his jacket. "See this rock? It's not five tons. It's more like eight tons. Five tons would be my height. I could put my arms halfway around five tons." Then, with an embarrassed half smile he added, "I can't move it."

"Well," I noted, "you can't leave it here. This is a common road, not my property."

"I could drag it up to the house, but that'll ruin your lawn."

"Hey, what's with a lawn," I came back. "We're talking art here. Let's do it!" I wasn't going to let the lawn stand in the way of my peace of mind.

And so the rock was lifted into the front loader until it fell out and dragged a bit, then again lifted and dragged up to the garage on our property. Amazingly, only a two foot path of grass from the gate to the garage was damaged.

Once again the excavator got down from the front loader for a conference. "If I put it on the cement, the weight may crack it."

"Go for it." My reply was inevitable.

The rock was moved onto the cement.

"Can you put it upright?" I asked, somewhat aware I was getting a bit demanding. "Yes," he said "but it may crash into the garage." I suggested he move it back a foot and try it.

It was the most amazing sight to watch. The rock was set upright and rocked back and forth about three times before it stopped dead, solid, powerful.

"Well, we're doing okay; let's put it into the garage," I suggested. Again, he offered a warning that it could nick the sides of the garage, but he would try. I helped guide it in. There was only about one inch of space to spare on either side. He did an amazing job.

"I'm working out my mid-life crisis," I said, trying to justify my relentless persistence.

"Can't you just make baskets?" he laughed.

Three years later my mid-life rock is still sitting only partially touched in the garage. Working on it with an air hammer causes strain on my wrists, so I cannot pot and chisel at the same time. After the mid-life energy passed, I decided to focus my time on pottery. The rock has become the butt of a few jokes. My neighbor has offered to take it out into a field and blow it up. But I know that it is not going anywhere and I'll get around to it when the time is right.

I found myself still confused about what had happened but filled with gratitude for the obvious deepening of experience that was taking place, and for the vehicle of my builder who, for whatever reason, had reflected this message for me. I was more aware than ever not to confuse the message with the messenger.

As often happens, a number of my clients reflected my own situation. They were women projecting their animus onto a certain man or men projecting their anima onto a woman. Because of my own experience I could listen to them with understanding and ask, "what is the gift they bring that would make you whole? Is that a gift within yourself that you have not claimed?"

> *Blaming and attachment to others is confusing the messenger with the message; it's a socially condoned cop-out that keeps us from the deeper spiritual and personal growth we are seeking.*

By October, all the ties and projections were finally dissolved. I was surprised that all of a sudden it seemed as if I didn't have to work on releasing them. They were simply gone. I remembered the feelings but did not feel them any more.

Astrological Reading

I sought out an astrological reading from a local woman and we soon became close friends. As she noted, the winter brought a time for much reading and meditation. I seemed to have an intuitive understanding of the unconscious as its contents broke into my conscious mind. The book *The Art of the Possible* by Dwana Markova, Ph.D. was fascinating and began to help me make sense of much of my summer experience. The book *Please Understand Me,* based upon the Meyers-Briggs ideas also helped make sense of my potential gifts and challenges as an intuitive feeler.

My astrologer lent me a copy of Barbara Hand Clow's book *Liquid Light of Sex, Understanding your Key Life Passages.* The book confirmed that my summer experience was what is referred to as mid-life crisis. The crisis is triggered by the position of the planet Uranus, as it moves for the first time directly across from the position it held at one's birth. This serves to open the flow of sexual energy through the root chakra. Some relevant snippets of her discussion on this subject:

"As the energy of Uranus Opposition flows into their root chakras, many people separate from the moralistic reality around themselves. Those with a blocked root chakra avoid parents, spouses, and other judgmental people as much as possible during mid-life crisis...

... the root chakra openings can break the blocks of sexual repression. This urge is a powerful one- the energy feels like a survival instinct to many blocked in the root chakra. At mid-life, disturbingly, suddenly the body seems to be on fire with a quaking energy that has no outlet....

A central issue for those with a blocked root chakra is trust. Once the Earth chakra has opened and we have conquered our fear of life, we need to trust others so that we can surrender to sensuality. That means becoming comfortable with ourselves and being able to reveal ourselves to another without feeling like we are being invaded or judged...

At mid-life, if you can totally trust just one other human, you will have begun to penetrate the repression that creates the block to sexual releasing. Our only access to the experience of trust is through other humans, and that experience may or may not be sexual.

As the kundalini energy rises, the extreme levels of sexual oppression ... engendered by a blocked root chakra, seem to force people into action. This is when counseling is needed, because taking action may often be the last thing one should do at this time...

One sure way to avoid transformation at mid-life crisis is to create a flurry of distractions, such as building a new house and decorating, getting another job, moving, or getting a divorce... Examining the inner issues will have been avoided the whole time!"[1]

Hand Clow's book made sense of my experience, and taught me that it was by no means unique. So, I was determined not to keep it quiet as if it were a source of shame, when so many others are or will be going through it too! Why do we hide it?

> *For me, honesty and openness about my mid-life conflicts allowed me to handle the situation with as much integrity as possible, receive support, and grow both sexually and spiritually.*

After reading her book, I reflected upon the responses of people with whom I had shared my mid-life experience before I even knew that Uranus had a hand in it. Some women were fascinated and envious of the energy. Others were fearful and warned me not to act on my sexual drives. Some encouraged me to follow my feelings and desires.

None of this advice helped me understand or resolve the situation. What I really needed and did not find was someone who could listen deeply enough to help me uncover my own wisdom, already waiting to be revealed within the depths of my own being. I needed someone who would facilitate my being present to the passionate feminine sexuality that I had repressed for so long. I needed Inner Listening.

---

[1] Clow, Barbara Hand. *Liquid Light of Sex: Understanding your key life passages.* (Santa Fe, Bear & Co., 1991, (p. 89-91). Reprinted with permission of the author.

Contrasting Dreams of the Animus

With the close of the influence of Uranus and my taking back my projections onto our builder came two contrasting dreams of my animus. The first one portrayed it as a devilish/comical character for which I felt both pity and raw attraction. It was a soft, grotesque, plastic male doll with large purple and pink bumps all over it. His penis was attached to his forehead. I told him that it didn't belong there and he moved it to his throat. I said it goes under the belly (which was quite substantial).

I could only describe my attraction to this ridiculous doll as raw and animalistic because even in the dream I couldn't figure out what I found so desirable. My dream ego was not the only one with this animus. With me were four other women, some younger and more innocent than my dream ego. Seeing them and feeling responsibility for them, I suggested that on the count of three we all shout, "go to hell!" We did and the dream ended.

I was lucky that I had a meeting with my friend that day. We were driving a short distance to check out a conference at a local resort. I shared my dream with her and she did an "if it were my dream" with it. We looked at how I was treating my animus. Could I claim the ugly doll as a part of myself or would I send it back into the unconscious to be projected once again? Sharing the dream helped me look at these questions and acknowledge these once hidden parts of myself. The comical and grotesque nature of the animus (not to mention the embarrassment of it) gave a flavor of humor and a sense of the ridiculous to what turned out to be a trip to check out a conference based upon false pretenses.

A week or so later I shared with my friend another animus dream. In the dream, I was in an empty room with a male figure. I was spinning and spinning. The male figure was Ken Wilber who, for me, represents compassion, love, wisdom and understanding. He was saying "Relax and fall in. Surrender, it's OK."

I was afraid that I would fall into him (which at the same time I desired). I was aware that I "should not" become one with him.

Then I woke up. The dream was an image of my animus that showed another, deeper, wiser, loving guide.

When I awoke, I had to ask myself where the "should not" response came from. Wouldn't it be the goal, after all, to be united with the animus, and integrate it into my life? Was there some part of me that feared this and is so conditioned that I do not allow to happen what I deeply desire and need for wholeness? And what about union with the grotesque animus? Was it not a sense of responsibility for the "others" that I felt I "should not" engage its primitive, raw sexually? What parts of myself are represented by those "others"?

The Bird on the Sign

Before I began staying home to write, do pottery and spiritual direction work, I was going to work at my sister's business while she had it in her home. I vividly remember making incense for an order and thinking with intense anger, "I shouldn't be doing this. I should be getting a Ph.D. or something."

To which I heard an inner reply, "You aren't in the present moment, are you?"

"No," I responded, "I'm too angry to get into the moment and that will just have to be okay I've taken notice, thanks."

When work was over I went home to our new two and one half acres of bliss, let the dogs out and walked around the back of the property that looks out on open fields and forest. As I walked along the fence line from one side of the property to the other I began to notice levels of "stuff", like energy, slipping off my outer energy field or aura. One, two, three, they released, each time bringing me more into the moment and more in touch with inner joy and well being.

When I came to the other side of the property, I saw an old weathered plywood board attached to a leaning post. At one time, it probably held a "Keep Out" sign, but now it was just weathered, simple and, to me, very beautiful. Sitting on the top of the sign was a little bird. I stood still, admiring the bird and sign, when I heard from within my head these words put to a song, "I'm glad you see it. I would have made it that way anyway, but I'm glad you see it too."

> We live so that God might see the world
> through our eyes.

I walked over to a tall clump of grass and cried. There was a sense of relief and awe and most of all, grace. I had been carried away in an emotion, now I was in the sacred grace of the present moment.

Letting Go and Allowing to Be

It seems that any time I am not honoring my spiritual journey, my dissatisfaction is projected on to a dissatisfaction with the spiritual journey of my husband. I see this projection all the time with premarital couples.

> When we are not walking our own soul
> path, we always seem to try to get others to
> improve.
> But once we are living the soul path, we can be
> happy to allow others to be where they are and
> may even see the divinity of another's way.

As I struggled to define my relationship with the church, I was also dissatisfied with my husband's spiritual journey. After all, when he left seminary, he seemed to leave everything. He could at least meditate! He did not seem to have a solid foundation. In reality, I couldn't perceive a foundation in him because I was out of touch with my own foundation.

What I began to realize was that I needed to let go. Let go of place, let go of Rev. status, let go of those outside affirmations that are not based upon my spiritual journey, but upon social and institutional legitimization. I was still making a last ditch effort to fit into the local Presbyterian structure, even though my ministry of spiritual direction seemed to fall outside of their scope of legitimate ministerial activities.

One day I had an out of town meeting with the, "Committee on Ministry", regarding membership in the local Presbytery. Attending were mostly middle aged to elderly women and men. They had a number of concerns regarding my ministry, such as, "You are working without church supervision and could become a cult figure!"

I said nothing but thought, "You seem to miss the fact that most ministers are cult figures and the church structure supports this."

They had no understanding about spiritual direction, letting go, or the soul path. They didn't know that in spiritual direction one is not trying to obtain power over others for the benefit of the institution or one's own ego. Rather, the goal is to empower others by encouraging them to walk their soul path, even if that path does not put them on the roster for further spiritual direction and help pay the bills.

Another concern was that I had a non-traditional ministry. Not too much I can do about that. And finally they were concerned that I was not attending the local Presbyterian Church. I explained that this did not nourish my spiritual journey, but volunteered to try to attend. They ended the meeting with the suggestion that I find a local church and for now remain a member of the Presbytery in California. I noted that this may be my only option at this point, but, that I am not in California now, I'm here.

Driving home I felt a sense of grief and loss. I no longer had a system of buddies and colleagues in the ministry. I no longer had a place in the church. Perhaps I no longer wanted a place there. But I still was grieving over the loss of what for so long had been my identity.

Once home, I began preparing dinner. Then the tears began to fall. No sobbing, just tears. Tears of release, tears of letting go.

I went and sat on the steps of the side door under an overhang where I could see Youngman in the yard hauling wheelbarrows full of branches he had trimmed from vine covered cedars. It was as if a veil had fallen from my eyes. All at once I saw him in his divine bliss. He was a monk, hauling wood and singing to himself. Only when I let go of my own false identity could I really see his true divinity.

> ❧ *Tears flow. Why? I don't know.*
> *Letting go, letting go of so much.*
> *Having nothing to replace it*
> *but the silence inside.*

In the fall I made an effort to keep my word and attend the local Presbyterian Church. Youngman would not go with me as he found worship superficial and self-serving. I felt an obligation to try it again. So one Sunday morning I woke up, got dressed and headed down the country road. But as I drove, I felt a lump in my throat. I did not want to go. It felt like a betrayal of who I am. So instead of turning right to go into town, I turned left to Fish Town and sat across from two charter boats tied up at the dock. I laughed softly to myself when I noticed their names. I was sitting between "Double Trouble" and "Infinity".

> *Off to Church?*
> *There really isn't much to say.*
> *It's just the way I decided to spend the day.*
> *I turned left instead of right.*
> *Went over by the docks instead of to church;*
> *to hear the rushing water and the occasional lurch*
> *of a fishing boat.*
> *And there, kissed by the sun and caressed by a breeze,*
> *I stayed out of the cold and found my true ease.*
> *And on a bench*
> *in-between "Double Trouble" and "Infinity"*
> *I received the courage to continue to Be.*

I reflected on how well this symbolized my life passion of bridging the secular and the sacred.

I tried attending the church again at a later date and did finally get inside the church doors, only to find what I already knew—I did not belong there. The service did do something for those who attended, but for me it seemed spiritually stale and, as Youngman said, superficial and self serving. I felt critical of it and guilty for being critical. Had I been in another interior space, I may have experienced it totally differently. But, in spite of the love and care and professionalism of those involved in the church, it just was not where I needed to be.

> *It is ironic that I left my ministry in order to learn to explore the unconscious.*
> *It was my hope and my goal to help the church heal from its deeply hidden wounds which function as barriers to our being the body of Christ—God's love in the world. Now, having acquired the tools to do that, I no longer fit in.*

During his life, Jesus was more concerned with the journey of the soul than with the well-being of the religious institutions of his day. But soon after his death, when Jesus became an institution himself, the driving focus was on upholding the doctrines which keep the institution in place, and the journey of the soul to love took a back seat.

Mindfulness

It was around this time that I read Jon Kabat-Zinn's book, *Wherever You Go There You Are.* I would read it in the mornings by the pond, taking time to just be with what was said and listen to it resonate within.

In the back of the book was an order form for mindfulness meditation tapes which I ordered and began to use. Mindfulness teaches us to observe our thoughts and feelings without grasping and getting caught up in them. So I spent time sitting and noticing, receiving the emotional awareness and growth I had so longed for.

Soon my sister's business was to move to a new set of buildings. It was in this new building that I experienced the contrast between being centered in the moment and being carried away (from my true self) by emotion.

By now, I was spending my mornings in mindfulness meditation and some time potting. It no longer felt good to me to be at the business all day; to do so was like a betrayal of my essence. So I would spend the morning in bliss, meditating and potting before the fireplace, then go in after lunch. I had a few direction clients by then and would see them in the mornings as well.

Often, by the time I went into work, I was quite centered. It felt as if I had two feet of peaceful space around me which nothing could penetrate. This particular morning was no different. While I was very focused, efficient, and present to my activity, a younger woman at the table began talking. She kept on chatting, as if her mind was bouncing off the walls. I realized that I too had often done this when working. I remained calm, simply observing what was happening. Her energy was agitated and ungrounded, but instead of affecting me, it seemed to bounce off that two-foot cushion around me. I felt no animosity towards her; in fact I felt no judgment at all.

I broke into a smile of appreciation at the realization of this. The fact that her banter did not throw me off center must have been noticeable because she said, "I'm not getting to you, am I?"

> 🍁 *The tolerance that allows others to be as they are comes when we are living from within our deepest self. Then no one has to live under false pretenses to try and "make" anyone else feel comfortable.*

During this time I was continuing to work on just being as I am. If I wanted to be accepted just as I was, this meant accepting others just as they are. More and more, as I went to work centered and calm, I would hear remarks like, "Are you okay?" or, "Perhaps you are manic depressive."

I was no longer bouncing off the walls entertaining everyone with erratic energy, reacting to where they seemed to be and trying to move them to a space that would be more comfortable for me.

> 🍁 *More and more I realized how important it is to accept people as they are, without judgment and without asking them to behave or feel differently so that I feel more comfortable.*

Each incident was a vehicle for helping me to understand myself better and be more faithful to my soul path. As one co-worker noted, "Everyone working here seems to be on a spiritual path. We're all learning, growing and healing." My sister, in her own special way, provided the atmosphere which allowed for such growth.

Taking Emotional Responsibility

I had a call from a woman who claimed that a man, let's call him Barney, was doing mind control on her. She was very angry over the phone and said that if I knew him I should tell him to stop.

After listening to about ten minutes of complaints, I finally asked her, "Do you want an appointment for spiritual direction or are you just calling to complain?"

Instead of answering, she continued to complain.

I told her, "You seem very hurt and angry, and it sounds as if it were directed to me."

She replied, "I'm sure the place where you meditate knows Barney and his mind control schemes."

"The place where we meditate has spiritual integrity," I told her.

She yelled, "I want some sacred space and I want to be honored!"

I had never heard the words "sacred space" and "honor" sound so foul. Her tone of voice made them sound like swear words. The contrast was almost comical. I asked her if she was honoring me and my sacred space right now with her phone call and her tone of voice. I suggested that until she learn to do that, she would find neither honor nor sacred space herself.

> ⚙ Blaming our actions, feelings or our life circumstances, or blaming others, is an attempt of the ego to protect its limited persona. Blame prevents us from taking responsibility for what we feel and how we respond to life.

If we have someone to blame, we are not responsible, because we are the "victim". The person who chooses to remain in a state of blame is not likely to seek help except to complain and try to change the one who is being blamed.

> 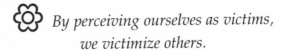 By perceiving ourselves as victims,
> we victimize others.

I don't know how this person's mental/emotional condition would be diagnosed by a professional, but it seems clear that until she stops being a victim and blaming/projecting onto this Barney fellow, she will find little relief from the hell of her own making. Nothing helps as long as one is not prepared to take responsibility for one's thoughts and actions.

Seek and You Will Find

> *There is nothing we seek*
> *which hasn't already been given to us.*

Doing spiritual direction—what I now refer to as Inner Listening—is like being present to someone who has been on a loop in the freeway, running around in circles for some time. They want to get off, change directions, find another way, but can't seem to find the exit. They come to direction to find the exit. What we discover is that the exit was always there, they just didn't see it. It is as if there was an old abandoned house in front of it and, because they associate the house with fears from the past, they never look closely at it or get near enough to see that the exit they seek is just behind it.

In direction, feeling safe and being in a non judging presence, they notice the house, and not feeling fear because they are in the present moment, take a closer look at the house, even walk inside to discover much more than we could ever imagine. They leave by the rear door and notice the sign for the exit they were looking for which is now accessible to them.

If I were to write a journal, an amulet to leave for future generations, hidden under my mattress or sewn within the sleeve of a coat, I would leave these words:
"Ask, and it shall be given you;
Seek, and you shall find;
Knock and the door shall be opened unto you:
For everyone that asks, receives;
And he that seeks, finds; And to him that knocks, it shall be opened."
But... that has already been said, hasn't it?

The ego's devices of moving us away from the inner experience of the soul and back to the justifications of the head are many. They take different forms for different people, but they all seem to involve judgment and fear of an experience. Some move away from feelings, others refuse to let go of feelings, and some avoid the nothing-ness—the void.
Had they stayed and surrendered to the experience, they may well have touched upon the Mystery we call God.

No one has ever yet come to spiritual direction without already having been given what they seek. It is like sitting in a restaurant waiting to order and unbeknownst to us a waitress puts a fresh, warm loaf of whole wheat bread on the table. Smelling but not seeing it we turn to our friend and say, "Gee, I'd really like some fresh whole wheat bread!" Our friend smiles and waits for us to notice.

The spiritual director is like that friend. It is the spiritual director's job to help people be present to what is hidden. He or she simply allows them to notice and 'be with' what they haven't been able to notice or 'be with' on their own.

 Life is a process of having been and becoming, in each moment.

When people reach a stage in their psycho-spiritual development where they need to seek out and live by their own inner authority and truth (the process of individuation), the church can act more as an inhibitor than an inspiration to growth. By its very nature, the church or any religious organization functions to sustain certain values and doctrines. When personal experience no longer can be contained within these, the faithful seeker must look elsewhere.

This need to look elsewhere can be a time of great loss as one lets go of the stabilizing factor of church with its routine and social connections. At the same time, letting go in order to seek a more flexible and appropriate life framework can be an exciting adventure.

Our ego, with its desire to maintain control, with its fears, goals, past/future orientation, opinions, judgments and conditionings, is a strong mechanism for maintaining our illusions of reality.

The question is, do we substitute one framework for another or do we discover our own inner truth upon which we compose our own belief system arising out of our experience of the Mystery we call God?

> ❀ *We seldom live in the present moment—the only moment when we experience God. As a result, when it comes to God, what we often create is a God of illusion, God created in our own image and likeness to service the ego and uphold our illusion of reality.*

> ❀ *To a great extent, the things we call evil and divine are but reflections of our inner shadow (unexplored, repressed parts of our self) and our inner divinity.*

Who is in Control?

In mid February, I was due to facilitate a retreat down state for 30 women. I was looking forward to it because it would be the first official activity I had undertaken since all the changes and since practicing mindfulness. I took along with me the mindfulness meditation tapes from Jon Kabat-Zinn which included an audio tape of random bells. I had read about using the random bells in a group situation in *Living the Mindful Life* by Charles T. Tart. Basically whenever a bell rings, the person speaking says, "the bell is ringing, be present."

I went there not only with lecture and discussion materials but with tools for meditation and ongoing mindfulness. The tapes would be a tool not only for the mindfulness and centering of the participants, but for my own as well.

The participants were from the town we used to live in down state. Ever since the planning of the retreat, I had been warned by the female pastor and some other women from the church: "Take control of this group. If things go too slow they will take over the leadership." Leadership, control. These were words right out of the old patriarchal model. I trusted that these were not going to be issues, at least not for me.

That evening, I began by facilitating a half hour lying down meditation which seemed very enjoyable to all the participants. Encouraged by the flow of silent breathing presence, I lengthened it to 45 minutes. This retreat was off to a good start and I knew that there was no need to worry about keeping their attention or seizing "control".

The next morning the pastor greeted me with: "O.kay, I am letting go of the control and putting this group into your hands.

"I smiled and said, "Okay."

For her, someone had to have control. I didn't tell her that I wasn't taking control, because this would allow her to relax and have some peace of mind. There was no need to try and move her from her position and ask her to feel differently.

For me, if there was any control, it came from the presence we call God. I was just going with the flow. The flow was heightened by the random bells which would periodically interrupt me mid-sentence to acknowledge the presence of silence. We added a deep breath of release to the bell sounds, and each breath moved us closer to our souls and the "Source" of our being.

During the discussion section I shared many of my personal spiritual growth experiences, among others the mid-life crisis, along with frameworks for understanding spiritual growth. There was a variety of responses from the women. Some were awed that one would talk so openly about "such things". Some admired my honesty and openness. Only a few thought it reprehensible.

I noted with joy that what others thought did not really matter to me. I was comfortable with my experience, my learning and the remaining mystery of it all. This level of comfort was new for me since I was so used to being a "People Pleaser".

Finally I had begun more fully to live from my own inner authority, honoring my deeper truth, and just being myself. In doing so, I could also honor others where they were, even if it was not where I was, without feeling defensive or threatened by it. That was one of the greatest gifts of the retreat experience for me.

Another gift came when one of the participants shared some Yoga movements with us. We were gathered around her in a circle. Suddenly she stopped and turned to me, tears filling her eyes. "There is so much love in this room," she said. We all took a moment to notice and savor the energy of love. We observed that it felt like gentle waves washing us.

It was significant that many of the retreat evaluations noted the greatest gift to the participants was the fact that I had enabled them to just be themselves. Weeks later, I was informed that at the sound of a phone ringing they were still taking a deep, silent breath.

> *Maybe God is simply asking us to grow, to Be, and along the way, to love one another.*

To Preach or to Be

Since my practice was new in town, the writer of the religion column in the local paper asked if she could come over for an interview. I agreed, our discussions were frank and at one point I shared that a healthy relationship with God grows and changes over time.

To give an example, I explained that I had come to an understanding about the teachings of Christ:

> **❰❰❰** *Jesus did not want us to worship him or regard him as an unattainable model. Rather, we are to learn from him and, through his teachings, enter into a relationship with the divine within each of us.*

So, over the years, I no longer experience Jesus so much as Lord and Savior, but more as a teacher and friend.

The columnist wrote that I do not experience Jesus as Lord and Savior but as teacher and friend. This of course raised the doctrinal ears in the church and I'm sure caused much discussion. The minister whose church I had lead in the 3-day retreat called back to say she had spoken to the Executive, and he had some questions about my Christology. She then suggested that I engage in some form of visible ministry to which they could relate.

Shortly after this discussion, I was asked to fill in one Sunday at the local Unity Church who had lost their minister some time ago. I preached once and they asked me if I would like to fill in for the next 6 months or until they called a new minister. I thought about it for some time and met with members of the committee.

As I was nearing a need to make a decision, I noticed that I had become anxious. What was going on? Why wasn't I looking forward to preaching?

I realized that I no longer wanted to push people into a different space within themselves, but to simply be with them where they are. I no longer wanted to preach Christ but to be Christ. At this stage of my life, ministry seemed like 'pushing' whereas spiritual direction work allowed 'being'.

I had to say no. I was letting go of the fact that ministry had to take place in the institutional setting of the church, under church sponsorship or within church doctrine. I was on a journey, a spiritual quest to live authentically from the soul, and I realized that the church could no longer fully support or validate my journey because part of this growth process is to trust the wisdom of the soul and surrender.

Accelerating Into Another Dimension— a Dream

> **❨** *The energies of the planets and constellations are reflections of different aspects of our self.*

One of the most powerful dreams I had during this time seemed to serve as a summation of the planetary influences that affected my journey. I was not really versed in the influences of the planets Saturn, Uranus, Mars or Pluto, but their energy was represented in my dream as aspects of myself. I took an interest in how our birth chart might reflect our soul path and affect our energies to confront and learn certain lessons.

No longer do I see competent astrology as pushing my boundaries, but as a tool for greater understanding of the personal and collective unconscious and the soul path. And although I do not have skills in astrology, I am blessed with friends who do.

In my dream, I was in a dark gray military jet fighter, flying in formation with other such planes. I was in the co-pilot seat, next to the pilot who was a dark skinned, large, energetic and powerful male who could have had the names Uranus, Pluto and Mars. He may have been all three in one, yet if there were a dominance of one over the others, it would have been Mars. There was no question that he was a competent pilot and I was content sitting in my place. In the middle behind us in the back seat was a skinny, white, nervous, conservative man who could only have the name Saturn.

Suddenly in mid-flight, the pilot began to accelerate out of formation. I noticed this but did not think too much of it until a female voice on the radio issued a warning, "You are accelerating at a high speed and are moving beyond this dimension. You will not be able to return." .

The pilot seemed concerned and asked, "What can I do?"

The tower replied, "There is nothing you can do except find a road and land."

At this point Saturn became very angry and said, "I knew I had to keep an eye on you!"

It seemed obvious that he had come just to do that! It was also clear that the three of us were going to be living in another dimension and Saturn was not pleased with that at all. At this point I turned around and said "Don't you see? This is God's way! You two never got along and now, for the next forty years you will be forced to be together!" For some reason, I was delighted with the prospect and the irony of it all.

I understood all the parts of my dream to be aspects of myself. It was a powerful dream that will no doubt reveal more of its meaning to me as years go by.

Facing the Inner Bear

 Isn't it interesting how some childhood

dreams still hold energy for us? Perhaps that is because they still have something to teach us about ourselves.

I was eight years old when I dreamed about going to the park to play. Soon after I passed the stone entrance, I looked to my left and saw a big brown bear approaching me from behind.

I began to run away and, realizing the futility of my actions, I heard a wise inner voice,

"Stop and face the bear."

I trusted the voice and stopped. Then standing face to face with this formidable creature said in my youthful way,

"Let's be friends!"

Whereupon the bear and I joined arms and went prancing down the hill, off to play.

The obvious lesson was that I should not be afraid to face my fears. With that lesson I forgot about the dream until it resurfaced with much energy at the age of forty-one to forty-two, the time of the writing of this book.

It felt as though the full message of this dream hadn't been realized yet. I stayed with the dream, looked up the native American meaning of a bear and found it to be a connector between heaven and earth, the same as my Myer-Briggs personality type.

To 'be' with this further, I began making clay sculptures of bears and as I was doing this recalled having made a clay bear when I was in grade school. It was big and chunky and rocked in a sitting position with etched hair all over it. As I sculpted the hulking, gentle creature with outstretched arms I noticed its wide belly which seemed to be its source of power.

I recall a martial arts teacher saying that women are lucky because our source of power is in our hips from which all martial arts movements originate. Interestingly enough, women are taught to hold this area in and not give it breath, but to breathe shallow from the chest. In doing so we are 'cut off' from our source of personal power.

I then realized that for me, the dream now told me that I needed to live from my inner power and trust my inner authority more. The bear became a sign of inner authority, personal spiritual guidance, and moving beyond fears. The dream still holds power.

Dreams of Snakes

One night I dreamed that I was walking down the sidewalk coming home from elementary school and heading towards the park (where I met the bear) from the other side. I looked down and saw a zillion black snakes. Some of these snakes had entered my right hip, and I managed to pull out a few.

I understood the dream to represent a poisonous energy that I had been holding in my hip. Not long after, a Jin Shin Do session cleared this energy and I had no arthritic pain or congested energy left in that area.

In the second snake dream. I had found a diamond backed brown snake and even though it seemed dead, my sister gave it a pill and I put it in a plastic bag in the refrigerator. Later that evening I went to the refrigerator to get a drink and noticed that the snake was moving inside the plastic bag. I wished had I used a zip lock instead of a sandwich bag.

I was very frightened and did not even close the refrigerator. I shut the door to my dogs room, realizing that would not really protect them from the snake entering then ran upstairs to wake up my parents. Dad woke up and I said, "Remember that beautiful snake I found?"

He nodded and I called out, "Well, it's alive!" He replied that we would have to notify the concierge.

Then I woke up. It seemed clear in the dream that what we were going to do was develop a plan to kill the snake.

According to some who follow Jungian psychoanalysis, dreams of snakes often represent our (individuation,) coming into being our own person. What part of me did I think was beautiful and acceptable when dead or sleeping but dangerous when alive and needed to be killed? What roll was the natural healer (my sister) in me playing that the rest of me was not ready for? What was I afraid of?

Part Three

Responding

Chapter 11

LESSONS IN MINDFULNESS

A Foundation For the Spiritual Journey

 Safety seems to come from being surrendered in the moment.

It is not unusual for us to note after a meditation session, that three fourths of it was spent with a racing mind where we grasped this or that thought and moved away from the present moment. However, noticing this and being willing to sit with a racing mind is in itself a sign of growth. I have always said that the "worst" (not that I judge!) meditation often informs my life the most, reminding me to let go and stop grasping so compulsively.

It seems that a mindfulness meditation session does not go by without someone mentioning that they were in touch with a sense of deep love, or of all that is. Mindfulness meditation is so simple and basic that it forms a strong foundation for the spiritual journey.

The reason for doing mindfulness meditation with others is that it serves as a half way house for being mindful in all aspects of community life. Some find that the energy of the group supports meditation more, because they are less easily distracted than at home. It's more tempting to get up and do the dishes or fix a dripping faucet when you meditate at home. In a neutral place, those escapes don't exist.

Meditation, especially mindfulness meditation, offers little ego gratification, easy answers or quick solutions, so it is not surprising that we often avoid, even discount or overlook the practice.

I was surprised to find that many Christians think that meditation is non Christian, even evil. Quiet sitting might seem evil when we become aware of the scary stuff inside that we have been avoiding.

> *If we would just sit with ourselves in the same love and compassion Jesus has for us, we might discover that what is inside is not so evil after all; indeed it is sacred.*

Our meditations reflect a lot about our lives and the baggage we carry. Our judgments and fear of the unknown, our need to fix, and our desire to be somewhere else do not just arise in our meditation but are burdens upon our everyday life. These burdens are the clouded perceptions and attitudes with which we meet ourselves, others, the world and the Mystery we call God. Every time we sit in meditation practice, we have the opportunity to notice how our baggage affects our experience of the present moment. And every time we get up from our meditation, we leave some contents of the baggage behind.

How Do You Justify Your Existence?

After I got through the more compulsive working mode I began to learn to honor the inner space where I needed to be. When I was tired I knew that I had a choice to drink coffee or take a nap. If I was thirsty I drank water, if I was hungry I ate and if I needed to write or just sit outside and marvel, I did that. It was becoming easier to "go with the flow." I decided that I needed to honor where I needed to be.

In some ways this was a luxury many desire but few say they can afford. But that is often just a convenient excuse, for even when time or money make it available, most do not notice or respond to the inner space where they need to be.

During this time I had an interesting meditation session which left me with an odd question: "How do you justify your existence?"

I knew that I don't have to justify it. But I also knew that I am conditioned to justify, and much of this is based upon productivity, not upon living the soul path which may involve not producing for a period of time. I think that I have justified my existence by helping (and to some extent pleasing) others. This would mean that if I was not helping (or pleasing) I should not exist.

Granted, there is nothing wrong with helping, but let it be done for it's own sake, not to justify existence. This would be self serving and probably not as helping as we had hoped. I wondered how many ministers justify their existence in the same way. Helping can then become almost a self serving compulsion that takes on the facade of a spiritual journey, but because it keeps deviating us from the empty space of just Being, may very well lead us away from the soul path.

> *There comes a time in life when, like Jesus,*
> *we need to go into the desert and just Be.*
> *Be with ourselves, the Source,*
> *our desires and compulsions*
> *and see them for what they are.*

The compulsion for "doing" is engraved in us through much social conditioning. We are valued when we are doing. Most doing produces clutter—stuff we really don't need in order to live and love fully. In our society we seem to justify our lives by our doing.

"What do you do?" we ask when we meet someone. If our "doing" is not meeting our needs, or if it does not reflect our deepest selves, we answer that question with an apology or explanation. And even if our doing is a reflection of who we truly are, we know that to answer with a job that pays little or has little status in society is not always comfortable. We judge according to our doing.

> ⌇ Somewhere we learned that we have to justify our
> lives by our doing. This message did not come from the
> Mystery we call God, the Source of our 'ising' and Being,
> but from the human ego's need to "be better than," to" win,"
> and to "be okay"
> when in the eyes of our creator we already are.

My Father's Death

A few months before his death, my father, who was a private pilot, flew me to the local airport near the area where I was to facilitate a retreat.

There was nothing unusual about the flight. I always enjoyed spending time with my dad and as usual was impressed with his expertise. One image does however stand out for me and that was his hands. I had no idea why, but when I looked at his gentle, big, strong, freckled hands, I was shaken by an overwhelming appreciation and love. I felt the urge to cry and realized that the feeling was connected to the eventuality of my parents' death. The moment passed and I focused once again on my retreat.

As I write this chapter, it is just a little over three months since my father died. On Father's Day evening, just after we kids left for our homes, dad took his dog out for a "walk" on a retractable leash while riding his bicycle. The dog's leash got tangled up in the bike. It is my husband's theory that dad pressed the front break, flew over the bike and landed on his head.

The injury did not seem bad at first; he even managed to walk back home. Mom drove him to the ER, from where he was helicoptered to the city hospital. However, the internal bleeding could not be stopped and caused pressure to build up in his brain. We were called to come at once to the city hospital near our home. I remember being in shock as the nurse related the news to me over the phone. I asked her, "Dad's dying isn't he?"

By the time I saw him the pressure had affected his body movements and his awareness of his surroundings. But he was strong as an ox when he gripped my arm, called me by my sister's name and asked, "Get me off the backboard; they've got me strapped!"

The male nurse immediately stepped in-between us, "I'm sorry, but we can't take him off until X-rays are taken." It was a painful scene and I felt helpless to have to watch it all.

Then the nurse said that my presence was causing him to be more active and suggested I leave. I stood outside the doorway and could hear him continue to speak and try to sit up.

Finally I couldn't bear it anymore, so I walked back in and asked, "Is he better?"

Dad was the same. I said with determination, "Since my dad is dying, I will be staying with him until our family arrives."

Enough bullshit. I knew where I needed to be and I made it clear. I was my father's daughter and I would be with him, just as he would have been with me if our role were reversed.

When the nurse finally left, my father calmed down and we were alone. Suddenly I thought I heard him call "Hey Juls!" from the near ceiling corner of the room, just in back of me. Holding his hand, I turned around and saw nothing but could sense that he was boxing at me from the ceiling corner. I laughed for a second because it was the last thing I would have thought about at that moment but the first thing dad would have done. Boxing was something we loved to do with each other. I'd egg him on until he produced a knuckle sandwich with my name on it. Then I'd run behind mom for safety. Dad was a good boxer in his younger days and he still had a strong body at age sixty-nine.

They finally took dad up for a C.A.T. scan and then hooked him up to oxygen, hoping to reduce the swelling. A half hour later a second C.A.T. scan revealed massive brain damage. I asked the neurosurgeon what he would do.

He responded frankly, "If it was my father and he had a good life, I would let him go."

I appreciated his honesty, but looking into his bloodshot eyes, I knew that the decision was ultimately ours to make.

We all knew my father's expressed wishes in his living will not to live as a vegetable. None of us wanted that for him, anyway. So my response was clear, "Then get him off those damn machines and let him die."

The family agreed and all but the breathing tube was removed. They had already begun morphine injections to reduce pain. He was then moved to the ICU.

After thirty-six hours dad breathed his last breath. We had thirty six hours to adjust to the fact that he would no longer be in our lives in the same way. Thirty-six hours to say good-bye and wish him all God's love on his soul's journey home.

Standing beside him I noticed his smooth, freckled, tan skin. My hand was on his shoulder at the time and for the first time, it occurred to me that my fair freckled skin had come from him.

These thirty-six hours were more than I had when I first encountered death some twenty years earlier. Then I was alone. Now I was with my family. At Philippe's death, I had been caught up by grief. With dad, the experience was different.

> *I felt grief but was also an observer of my grief. I remember standing at the foot of my father's bed and feeling like a mountain. Rooted, centered and connected at the base to my father and to my family and to the sacred source of all that is, the Mystery we call God.*

Not too long after this inner observation, a friend of my dad's came in and said, "You look so serene!"

At one point, I sat in the room with a woman who was a dear family friend, when I noticed a lot of light bodies in the room—no shapes, just faint, elongated pulsating lights. It occurred to me that dad's mom, and some other souls dear to him, were also present in the room. I walked over to the friend, whose husband, dad's best friend, had died seven years earlier. I was about to say "I think your husband is here," when I choked up. She then looked up and whispered to me, "You know, I have the feeling that my husband is here!"

Perhaps the hardest thing about a parent's death is witnessing the grief of the surviving partner. Mom sent each of us home once, but she did not leave his bedside. She hardly ate or slept. It was about the thirty-fifth hour when my sister and I could almost hear dad say, "Don't love this to death, let's get on with it." I had hardly said, "I think we should remove the breathing tube," when she nodded as if thinking the same thing. Dad wasn't one to love things to death. Dad was a pilot. A good one. He wasn't one to linger on the ground when he could be flying, and we knew that he had a lot of new space to explore. Who were we to hold him back?

Father officially died two minutes after the breathing tube was removed. His last breath left in a loud "oaah." His spirit seemed to fully detach as his jaw dropped, and the body lying there was no longer my dad.

Dad's body was cremated. Youngman and a dear neighbor on our road made a box out of cherry wood that was given to us by a talented local woodworker who went to the same church as my parents. I wood burned dad's name, grapevines and all the things dad enjoyed onto the outside of the box. Inside we placed his ashes.

I was leading the memorial service together with mom's pastor. The evening before the memorial I went for a walk alone. I had put on dad's jean jacket which still seemed to hold a lot of his energy. At one point during the walk I realized that I was talking to him and it seemed clear that he wanted me to thank his friends for coming to the service. I agreed to do that for him. That evening as I lay in bed I had the sense of an energy over me. It was an energy other than mine and I decided to just accept it, since all is of God. It lowered into my space and the next thought I had was, "So this is what it is like to be my daughter!" I laughed because dad seemed to always be amused by me and perhaps he did wonder what it was like to be his daughter!

The memorial service went very well, though it was hard to look at his friends or my family. I think everyone left with a sense of the love dad had shared in his life and a remembrance of how he had touched them personally. We were touched by the value of life and the awareness that our time to go could come as suddenly as his. My husband drove my mother back to the house and my sister went back with her partner. I stayed to greet dad's friends and I received much love and many hugs.

> *The only thing nice about a funeral, I used to say when serving the church, is that we are one in our need: To grieve and to celebrate the life of the one who died.*
> *Our barriers are down, and we are being 'real'.*
> *Grief has a way of facilitating this.*
> *Death, the great equalizer.*

My father's death reminded me of how fragile this phase of the soul's life is and that I need to be about who I am.

Beyond Fear—Exploring the Camp

Youngman and I arrived at the camp amid countless warnings of bear, raccoon, skunk, porcupines and bad weather, not to mention the overgrown road blocked by numerous fallen limbs which would alone take a few hours to clear! But fear tends to exaggerate reality and the road was indeed overgrown but not impassable.

We spent a few hours pitching the tent and digging the latrine hole, when I noticed that the afternoon sun was about as warm as it was going to get, so I announced that it was time for our baptismal swim. We undressed and after our "ritual of hesitation dance" dove into the cool golden water. Our dogs, Noon-sup and Girl, followed suit. Youngman had sighted some old weathered logs and pointing over to the near right hand edge of the lake, he suggested that we swim over to them.

> ☙ *At first I hesitated. After all, there might be*
> *icky, slimy branches under the water!*
> *Then, noticing my fear, I tossed it off and*
> *jumped in.*
> *Suddenly the beauty of the moment opened up*
> *like never before.*
> *I was struck with the realization of how limiting*
> *fear was to my experience of life.*

Swimming towards the logs I cried out, "This is better than Tarzan and Jane!" Indeed. Sitting naked on the old silver log we became one with the golden waters, the grasses surrounding the edge of the lake, and one another. "All the things I miss because of my fears," I kept saying to myself.

Ever since I had been coming to this camp as a little girl, this place has held me in mystery and a touch of fear. I couldn't help but notice that the mystery and fear seemed to be replaced with a new found desire to explore these sacred surroundings. My perceptions were changing. Even the drive to the camp from the town seemed only a short distance longer than the drive from our house to the city and certainly the roads to the camp were newer and better than the ones we have at home! And yet, I had always lived under the illusion that the camp was far away from civilization and that this made it difficult to live there year round.

I wonder what connection this has to the unconscious. I have always identified the camp as my "sacred space" where I was more in touch with my unconscious, my soul. Now, in my later years, I explore the mysteries of the unconscious with more ease and certainly less fear than ever before, and I facilitate this in others as well.

Perhaps my relationship to the camp is but a reflection of the sacred space within.

I ask myself then, is there anything that blocks me from living fully in the camp right now? My answer was that I still have a need to plan for satisfaction for the future. The camp is very much in the moment. One serves the fears of the ego, the other is love.

◌ If I were to live up here
I would not be someone important.
I would wood burn dragonflies
and water lilies
and hold a toad now and then.

I would marvel at the beauty of what already is,
now, in this sacred moment.

I would make a pot or two,
and I would write
just because the vessel and the word merge the
inner and the outer
and come as gift.

And if God is willing
I would walk with others on their sacred path.

And once in a while when I jump out of the
moment,
I may look back with regret or question the
choices I made.

Could I have been somebody after all?
A peacemaker at the UN?
Pastor of a big church?
A Jungian analyst?
A Ph.D.?

Until a dragonfly whisks it's wings past my ear,
or a fish jumps
or a bird sings
or a beaver slaps it's tail at the sight of an
approaching dog,
bringing me back to the moment
here and now.

No, I could have been somebody
but instead
I chose
to be me.

The Power of the Present Moment

There is something about mindfulness and growing in it that makes even the worst argument somehow acceptable to be with.

I was having a blissful compassionate day. I was a powerful, radiant woman, and it did not seem to matter what the circumstances were. They were not good. It was early winter and the roads were very slushy. My tires lost contact with the pavement and I began crossing the country road sliding sideways. Ahead of me were an oncoming van and a telephone pole. Prepared for the worst, I laid down over the passenger seat, covered my head and offered myself to God. My car spun around and — "thud!" — all I hit was the snowbank. I went to a nearby home to call a tow truck and after being pulled out, bought new snow tires. I felt very blessed for all the help I received from the man who welcomed me into his house to the tow truck driver to the tire sales man. I was still blissful.

When I returned home to share my adventures and "near death" experience, my husband was angry. I hadn't consulted him before purchasing the expensive tires. Standing at the kitchen sink, I was feeling regret over my actions when suddenly I caught inner visuals of a dark puff ball in the unconscious releasing a squirt of its contents up into my conscious mind. With that I had the most awful feeling that formed itself into these words, "I shouldn't have had a good day today."

But the contrast between the day when I was moving, radiating and relating from my inner source of strength, love, joy, beauty and self-worth contrasted so sharply with this constricting feeling of "I'm a bad girl" that I took notice. "My God, where did that come from? No, it doesn't fit! That's a bunch of garbage. What is happening now has no effect upon what happened earlier, nor should it."

Then I began to 'be' with this old stuff I had noticed. I realized that a year ago when we had such an argument, I had probably released the same unconscious material into my mind but really bit into it, really believed it! What was it? The contrast between the blissful day and the moment it all burst asunder stayed in my mind. It seemed to be saying not only that I shouldn't have had a good day but that I shouldn't have lived out of my inner source. It was my inner source that was really being attacked.

Just a few days earlier, during a direction session, I had asked a client if she noticed a difference between an example she gave of trusting her inner source and living from it and not trusting it. I was trying to help her see the contrast in clear examples so when it happened again she would take notice. And, as often happens, now I was the one taking notice!

The Inner Death Penalty

> ℰ𝒳𝒪 The punishment for not pleasing others is the sentence of death to the inner Source of power and radiance.

The next day was Sunday and after meditating, I sat with this new development. The evening before my husband and I were watching a movie on TV about someone wrongly sentenced to death for a murder he did not commit.

Somehow during the meditation I became aware that the punishment for not pleasing others is the sentence of death to the inner Source, my power and radiance. This is probably particular to intuitive feelers who are always attentive to pleasing others. But it is also what society teaches. If you do not live by our rules, you die. In some countries not living by the rules can be as simple as holding other religious and political beliefs. Somewhere I read about an idea I knew to be true:

> ❧ All people are searching for love, even those who are so wounded and misguided as to murder. It makes no sense to respond to such a need with equal or more violence.

> ❧ Having the death penalty in our society teaches us unconsciously that when we break the rules or do not please, we should die.
> Most of us are sentencing ourselves to capital punishment by losing touch with who we truly are.

Bliss

> ❧ There are times, like right now, when I feel blissful. All is coming together to be perfect in the present moment.

I often explain these moments by saying that I could die and be in heaven. What I feel is immense gratitude for life in its completeness. It is the way the end of my braided hair curls around my neck, the loose connection of my clothing, the breeze blowing through the kitchen window, the sense of oneness with the garden from which I just picked lettuce and spinach.

I move easily into my Tai chi/ballet/yoga movements, feeling the muscles, relishing the balance and awareness. I could have melted into my dogs—so precious, so themselves. I relish their smell, the way they move their heads as they watch the early morning breeze ripple on the pond. The breeze speaks of rain and the transitional weather causes me to suspend definitions and just be present. I get a lump in my throat. I am on holy ground.

> *There is a completeness even in the midst of my incompleteness.*

I remember an odd thought as I once took the dogs on our morning walk in the snow. Noting the beauty of the dogs as they stuck their heads into the fresh snow, smelling the scents beneath and coming up with snow puffs on their face and nose, I remarked to them that, if they knew how beautiful they are, they would simply become bliss. Then it occurs to me that this is what they already are.

> *When we walk our soul path, we become more at one with the energy of our Source, the Mystery we call God. Then, the earth and all her creatures manifest this oneness to us.*

It is we humans who have the ability to separate from bliss and ultimately from the Mystery we call God. It is the human mind that categorizes, separates, judges, struggles to change things and takes us out of the present moment.

If we become like the land and sea and all her creatures—then we live in a state of being that is at one with all there is, neither good nor bad, simply bliss.

> *All things originate in the Mystery we call God, the Source. It is we who divide and separate things, determining their value according to how they serve or do not serve our illusion of reality.*

Chapter 12

RESPONDING WITH OTHERS

From Isolation to Creativity

Winter has a way of bringing about a sense of isolation in the north. Tourists or "fudgies" as we call them have gone south along with the summer residents or "snow birds." There are only three houses on our dirt road where people live year round. It's always a pleasure to stop and talk with a neighbor or wave as I pass them on the road. But isolation is more than not having neighbors! For a person such as myself to whom career is so important, professional isolation can be devastating. Add to that the mid-February discontent we in the north seem to catch, and it's a mixture for trouble, change or a trip to someplace warm!

My sense of isolation always seems to come at this time of year and I notice that I tend to be out of the moment, unhappy with where I am. This never happens in any other season. In spring or summer I sit by the pond to my hearts content, do my pottery work, writing, see clients. I am so happy I dance around. But late mid winter brings discontent.

No wonder the north is industrialized. Isn't industrialization the sign of discontent with things as they are, a need to be somewhere else in terms of technology, discoveries and success? I often wonder whether there ever would have been a need for industrialization if we were truly able to live in the moment. Would it even exist? And, if not, how would we use our creativity, living in the moment? I then realized that I needed to do just that—use my creativity instead of dwelling on the restlessness.

What to do? I had a dream of a space in town where I could have my practice. However, this did not seem financially feasible and I didn't care to raise my hourly rates.

Despite this obstacle, I decided to share my dream with my friend who owns the local metaphysical bookstore. She immediately noted that lots of people were talking about a need to form a natural healing center in town. So, just for fun, we looked up some local properties that were for sale.

A few days later I shared the idea with a local yoga teacher. It just so happened that at the time I called her, she was envisioning what she wanted in a healing center! Our very fruitful conversation led to a few meetings, where other interested people were soon to join.

At first our attention was on getting a space where we could have our practices, a health food restaurant, bookstore etc. Then, eventually we realized that what we desired and what seemed to be happening was not so much a place as an association. And so, Natural Healing Way—"a loving association of healer and holistic resource persons dedicated to exploring, guiding, enhancing and empowering the natural state of wholeness in the life of the individual and the community"—was formed.

From my own limited perspective, I couldn't have dreamt up a way to realize my desire. Little had I known that God's plan was much grander; all I needed to do was take that first step and trust that I would be led in the right direction.

Success is Simplicity, Honesty, Truth and Love

One day I spent time reviewing what is important to me. I value simplicity, honesty, truth and love. Maybe valuing these things means not playing the "games" of the world—be it the game of spiritual materialism, or of disempowering, or of teaching and selling mindfulness in unmindful ways. I guess I will have to find my own way of being in the world but not of it.

I certainly have chosen a good life partner to help keep me simple, honest, and loving as I seek to live my soul path. If he didn't bruise the ego's pride, I wouldn't be aware of how much I rely upon it instead of following the soul's path. Sometimes we confuse one for the other.

I find that there are some clear differences between the ego's pride and the path of the soul:

> *Pride wants us to make our mark in the world. Soul wants us to learn, grow and love. When pride falls, it falls hard and makes a lot of noise. Soul, on the other hand, is quiet, warm, comforting, glowing and just knows on a deeper level. Pride wants acknowledgment, reward and recognition. Soul is its own reward. With little effort, the fires of the soul consume the green wood of ego's pride.*

Perhaps our minds confuse our will and satisfaction with the will of God. In some way, I had defined success with God's will—being part of the spiritual success movement, making a big splash, being somebody. This is the path of the Pharisees. I prefer the narrow path, the path of constant letting go of those things which pull me out of the wisdom and love of my soul where I am more in touch with the synchronicity of life and the love of God.

> *For me, the inner and the outer have to match. To do otherwise would be like selling my soul—or sacrificing the process for an unworthy goal. For me, peace only comes when I align my life with my soul.*

Where is the Monk on the Hill?

It had been almost ten years since I visited Korea and our in-laws, so Youngman and I decided to take that long overdue trip. I wanted to do one special thing which Youngman had to promise—I wanted to visit the monk on the hill.

Not much had changed except that the children in the village had grown, as had the village. No one at the health center remembered where Monk's Hill was and the city had changed so much that the roads didn't look familiar to us anymore.

> Seeking the monk on the hill,
> we got lost in the sights and sounds of the city.

It seemed that a whole nation was lost in the city. I marveled at how odd it was that the Buddhist way of simplicity and mindfulness is growing strong in America while getting lost in Korea.

Youngman describes the atmosphere of Korea as having the energy of chaotic economic growth. Money is the motivating factor for just about everything. This might be great for investors but I wouldn't want to live there anymore, and neither would Youngman. We had been offered jobs teaching at a rural college but refused to even consider the offer.

I think that the realization that he would not chose to live in Korea again was a difficult one for him. Before, that was always an option. Now it was not. I asked him, "What effect does this have on you?" He said, "It makes me more committed to being where I am now."

We never did find the monk on the hill.

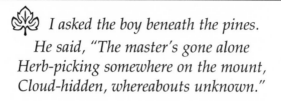 *I asked the boy beneath the pines.*
He said, "The master's gone alone
Herb-picking somewhere on the mount,
Cloud-hidden, whereabouts unknown."

Chia Tao (777-841) Trans. Lin Yutang

Is-ing

More and more I was experiencing myself in the world as if I were living at the camp—on sacred ground. There were fewer highs and fewer lows—more of a simple, peaceful being or 'is-ing'. I didn't have a desire to be anywhere but in the unfolding moment. The effect of this was that I could not prioritize or be future-oriented.

A friend once challenged me, "Do you not trust yourself to make decisions and priorities?"

As I replayed that statement in my mind, I recognized an underlying assumption that decision-making and prioritizing is necessarily good, and not to do so implies a lack of trust in Self.

So I replied, "I trust myself not to make decisions/priorities."

 I prefer to trust the moment.

To brush my teeth or admire a toad is the most important thing I do when I am doing it. Not forcing or wishing myself to be where I am not is the most important thing I can do right now.

One of my favorite stories is that of a beggar in India who sat and begged in one place all his life, seeking to be rich but dying poor. When the townspeople buried him in the spot where he was begging all his life, they discovered he had been sitting on the treasures of a king.

> *What if we allow ourselves to be exactly as*
> *we are — right here and now?*
> *What if we accept things exactly as they are —*
> *right here and now?*

So many people get scared that if they meditate they will become nothing and lose themselves. They do indeed lose something—the compulsive drive to move away from themselves. What would it be like to just be here now?

For me, it means to be with the pond and its critters, or to be with the cup I am pulling up without having my mind off in fantasy conversations. It means to be so present with a client that nothing matters but what is happening here and now.

What would the world be like if we didn't feed the sense of dissatisfaction that seems so ingrained in us? Would bigger be better? Or would we begin to see what is around us and in us? Would we shed our dread and once again wake up each morning in child-like wonder and excitement?

> ᕟ *This strange new emerging awareness*
> *of being in the moment defies description*
> *and if I didn't trust the source,*
> *I would move away from it too.*
> *But that may be more and more the gift emerging.*
> *I do not have to move away anymore*
> *or bounce off the walls.*
> *I can be with myself where I am*
> *and go deeper into the mystery. And so too with*
> *others. This is gift. It is 'ising'.*
> *It is what I have prayed for and must have known*
> *was inside as sure as the source of life in us.*

Return to the Pulpit

Once, after service at the church my mother attended, I walked over to the lectern and looked out into the sanctuary. There was a strange but most comfortable feeling that came over me and the phrase "this is good" that went along with it. A month later, I was asked to preach there, as the pastor was not well. I readily accepted the invitation. I worked into the service a story I had written, called "The Four Apple Trees".

> ᕟ *It was a story about stopping the battle, letting go into what is, loosening our judgment and accepting ourselves and others just as we are. In doing so, we discover tremendous gifts in what we once feared and judged.*

There I stood in front of the congregation where I had officiated at my father's funeral service. I felt no boundary, no resistance or defensiveness from either myself or the congregation, just a clear flow of being.

The congregation was visibly enjoying the story. A deep feeling of connection with them allowed me to ad-lib so that they could participate in the telling. At one point I could feel the heat rising from the collective body, both emotionally and physically. People were actually perspiring. After worship, I was the recipient of much love and many hugs. It occurred to me that there was a bodily release of energy, a cleansing of some sort taking place that account-ed for the heat and the feeling of love surrounding us.

Interestingly, what happened in the worship mirrors what hap-pens in Inner Listening sessions. We all have stories of conflict, trau-ma, or other unresolved issues which left us wounded. By being with the story in an atmosphere of love and acceptance, we deepen into our wounded spaces, until we feel loved and accepted in these wounds. This piques a physical release of blocked energy, as the energy is no longer stuck in one place to protect that wound. The result is an all-pervading feeling of love, peace and contentment.

To 'Be' With our Feelings

"I really enjoyed interviewing your husband at the radio show the other day; it went very well," I said.

I was feeling good about the two interviews I had done with a local professional for the public radio interview program I volun-teer to do, called "Heart to Heart."

"Yes," she answered, "he enjoyed it too and thought the first interview went well, but he wasn't sure about the second one."

My guts wrenched and a stabbing in my solar plexus almost felt as though "the wind was knocked out of me."

"Oh. my God," I thought, "I talked too much and didn't give him a chance to say what he had to say in the show. This isn't good. I need to 'be' with this feeling and I'm not looking forward to it!"

I went home early to 'be' with the feeling in my solar plexus, but I managed to avoid it until evening. At eleven o'clock, when my defenses finally ran down a strong, sudden sensation welled up in my solar plexus, and I knew I had no choice but to go into the meditation room and listen. I lay down on the floor and prayed for help while 'being' with this familiar yet scary feeling in my body.

The feeling was manifesting as a strong self-loathing. As I stayed with it, I observed that it came from the same place where I used to try to diminish my power as a child when I was scolded.

I observed it unfold more. I remember being busy playing in the living room and not saying hello when my father came home.

My mother scolded me, "You hurt his feelings. You'd better apologize."

I felt awful and apologized to my father. The idea that I could have such power was confusing, especially since I hadn't intentionally done anything. During my bath that evening I would be filled with self-loathing and try to diminish my power at the power center, my third chakra. It's interesting that, even as a little child, I instinctively knew that this was a storehouse of personal power.

Was there more to this? As I recalled this memory, I allowed my imagination to play with it. Did I say something snotty to my Dad and that got me in trouble? What would it have been? The words, "Well, you're never home anyway," came rushing in.

"Oh my God," I realized, underneath all that self-loathing lay a sense of loss of relationship with my dad because he was often out of town working. A few tears ran down my cheeks. The wrenching feeling in my solar plexus was gone. I smiled to myself. I had finally allowed myself to feel what had been to frightening to feel as a child. From the age of twelve I carried this fear of my power and self loathing around.

Finally, at forty-four, I was free to live without it.

> As a child, I was unable to separate behavior from essence. If I did something wrong, I must be bad. But this was not the intent of my parents or anyone else. It was just the misinterpretation of a small child. It was my behavior which was being corrected, not my essence.
> Suddenly I was filled with an awareness that my true identity was simply love.
> "I am love."

Do Unto Others...

A man was yelling ten inches from my left ear and pointing his finger in my face. It turns out that he was angry over the actions of someone else which he felt I should be responsible for.

Afterwards, while trying to throw pots on the wheel, I found myself in a constant inner debate, yelling at him, that he should treat others as he wants to be treated himself. As I moved from taking offense to understanding the type of thinking that would encourage his behavior, I realized that such behavior comes from old wounds and fear.

I talked it over with a few friends and found that talking helped me get more perspective and be more centered with it. But I still found myself preaching a sermon to him in my head as I was working on my pottery.

Later, I was rereading the booklet *Your Owner's Manual* and came again to a passage of profound depth:

 Teach no one that they have harmed you.

Your Owners Manual, Burt Hotchkiss

I sat with this idea and reflected on how in retelling my story a few times I was asking for confirmation of my victimhood. I'm good, he's bad. A lot of bunk. What was I hoping to get from this? What in myself was I avoiding?

After a few more days of staying with this feeling, I felt a shift. I can only describe it this way:

> *My love for this person did not allow me to be a victim because in being a victim I am holding him responsible for my wounds, and I am claiming myself to be powerless.*

I did not want to knowingly hold anything over another person. I did not want any harm to come his way. I wanted him to just be himself. I wanted him to be blessed. I am not powerless. I do have choices.

The most crucial realization was this:

> *At the time, I may have had no choice about being treated unfairly.*
> *But now, I do have a choice about how to 'be' with this experience.*

I wanted to learn to be more mindful and observing in all situations, even ones where I feel 'threatened'.

How often I've seen clients who were abused as children perpetuate the cycle of abuse by their choices as adults, because they see themselves as powerless victims. Their healing, not unlike mine, is moved along when they realize that being a victim no longer serves them.

> *Victimhood serves the ego and false persona. It does not serve the true emerging self—the soul.*

How can I be with all this? Taking a deep breath and seeking an answer to my question, I open a book on the spirit of religions and come to an old proverb:

 "Be like a tree which covers with flowers the hand that shakes it."

—Japanese proverb

Perhaps it is time for me to let go of the pain, anger and victim mentality. Perhaps it is time to reclaim my own power, my own voice and honor the motivation to love, share and enable others to live their soul path. Doing so is consistent with the message, knowing that I too unmindfully fall into some of these worldly traps. There but for the grace of God....

Shadowy Figures

I had been feeling bloated all day—physically and emotionally. In the evening, at the opening of my meditation, I prayed for guidance in understanding the symbolism of that feeling. Was I taking in too much? Then, after a short meditation period, I went to bed. That evening I woke up with the image of a dream still in my mind.

In the dream I looked out of my window and noticed three people walking the length of our property. Ever vigilant, I decided to let them know they were trespassing. When I called out I noticed that behind them, among the trees, were many sinister shadowy figures nimbly moving about. I was in trouble now. Had I just let them go by, they would not have noticed me, but now I had called their attention. They looked as if they were going to approach the house. Filled with fear, I called my two dogs to attack. The dogs did not do as I requested.

Then I woke up. It seemed that I had an option with these shadowy parts of myself. I could get their attention and try to fight them or let them pass by. It felt safer not to face them and hope that they would go away.

Then again, would ignoring them really bring me safety? After writing out the dream, I began a poem and was surprised to see where it led:

Shadowy figures in my dream
odd reflections of who I am?

Nimbly leaping
ever treading
on my serenity.

Who are you so bold as to pass
so close to the house where I live?

Powerless in my fear,
I ask the dogs to attack.
But they hesitate,
do they know?
One cannot pounce
on a shadow?

I think instead
I'll give a party.

Oh shadowy figures
come closer, please,
let's take a chance,
that I might learn
your nimble dance!

After the poem, I realized that my first twilight response to the dream had been fear-conditioned. This is a very common literal response to dreams which people often have and which they often are reluctant to give up.

We have options on how to receive the fear of an unpleasant dream:

Deplore it—call out the dogs to resist and attack.

Ignore it—hope that by not dealing with it, it will go away.

Explore it—not take it so literally, put the fear in perspective and find the gift of the dream.

Chapter 13

MOVING OUT INTO THE WORLD

There is no Problem; You Made it up

I had the honor of working with a client who got to that special place inside herself where the line between the Mystery we call God and the self is blurred. In the session, she went into a dark cave lit by candlelight and discovered a beautiful place within herself. She saw herself free and pure, without all the encumbrances she usually carries with her in day-to-day activities.

And then she saw an angel. It was a magical creature —happy, peaceful, full of love. "What took you so long?" the angel asked as if to imply that she had always been there. I asked her if the angel had a message for her. The angel told her,

> *"There is no problem; you made it all up. You chose to see it that way. You chose your perception, and you can choose another."*

It was a treat to sit with her while she was with the angel, because she was experiencing herself without all the incumbrances she had grabbed in life, which kept her from being her divine self. I knew that the message she received was for me as well.

The Nut Within

In his work *The Soul's Code,* James Hillman refers to the soul as an acorn, a potential oak tree within each one of us urging us to grow and live our unique calling.

The book must have had some impact upon me, as the next day, I woke up early to the light of a bright waning moon with that familiar sense of my own acorn calling out to me, deeply rooted into the earth and growing more and more each day into a beautiful, strong tree.

Lying in bed by the light of the moon, I reflected on the pull of the soul and the course I had taken in honoring it. It seems that, so far, there were three steps to this process:

 First of all, grow emotionally and develop healthy boundaries.
Second, be present in the moment and experience the wonder of life around us—claim the value of simply 'being' instead of doing.
Third, trust love while in the presence of Self and others.

I reflected on the way my work in the church and with clients has facilitated this evolution. I could see, for a moment, how my gifts come together for a purpose greater than their individual parts. I could see how there is still growing and letting go to be done before the call of that nut within would feel satisfied and complete.

The paradigm shift as manifested in my inner and outer life was taking place and was not yet finished. Perhaps it never will be.

Maybe the desire to have a solid paradigm for life is part of that old model of needing to have rigid answers in a world that is but a constant transformation of energy.

Things seem to be coming into place. Each lesson has not just its own value but value in the context of the whole as well.

Just as the pieces are forming in the jigsaw puzzle of my life, so I am but one piece in the jigsaw puzzle of existence. And perhaps, my piece, just like yours, is essential to the whole picture.

The Significance of Rituals

"Free Spiritual Healing", it said on the sign at a booth at a local alternative health fair. The two practitioners had on white lab coats and were very noticeably serene as they did energy work. Somehow it felt very phony to me. I was aware that this did not seem to be bothering anyone else and wondered what was being triggered inside of me. Their work was probably wonderful, and I didn't want to judge them.

At another booth, a woman wearing large bangle earrings was doing some trade marked energy work on a man seated in front of her. She was projecting a strong personality while moving her hand around the third chakra area. She had as much noticeable drama and movement in her style as the former couple had serenity. She too was probably achieving the wanted effect, but I was struck by the drama of it all!

I wondered if Jesus would have exhibited here, and decided he would have been outside just visiting with and loving people.

The next day I sat and reflected. I wondered if we are not like someone who is supposed to plug in a cassette player (the client). Some of us put on fancy clothes, some kneel, pray and dance, some move violently. We think that these rituals have power in and of themselves, but they don't. My response to all of this is "Get out of the way and just plug the darn thing in!"

Ritual has an important place and I don't think there is much we humans do that is not ritual. But when someone needs to be connected to the Source, we really might be better off to facilitate it with as little attachment as possible.

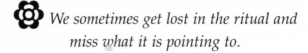

We sometimes get lost in the ritual and miss what it is pointing to.

I shared this with a wise woman who comes to meditation and she told me a story. She once spent a week at an ashram. During her stay, she was assigned laundry duty, and given specific instructions. Soon someone else walked in and told her she was not folding the laundry right, and showed her another way. Then another person came in and told her to do it another way. A fourth person came in with a different method. Each person sincerely believed that theirs was the right way and that it really did matter how the sheets were folded.

A few weeks later she entered nurses' training. A young man was their instructor for the morning. He welcomed them and said: "The first thing I am going to teach you this morning is the proper way to fold a sheet." My friend said that she broke out in laughter. "I really didn't think," she said, "That there was yet another way to fold sheets!" The teacher, however, did show them yet another way!

My observation of the health fair brought home a message which I need to keep foremost in my life:

> *Stay at the core. Don't get lost or hung up on ideology or technique. God is much greater than that.*
> *Be present in love. Get out of the way.*

As I negotiate with a publisher and realize that I will have much responsibility for marketing this book, I am apprehensive of the theological and ideological criticism I might receive. But all I can do is come from the core and speak my truth. It need not be anyone else's. There is no need for battles and certainly no need to join the carnival.

Someone once pointed out:

> *Some people need a ritual for permission to enter into union with God.*

If we need permission, then is there some conditioning we have that tells us it's not okay to be there? Where does the permission come from? We often think it comes from an outer authority but it really comes from our own soul seeking constant union with the Source/God.

> *Where is the message that it's not okay to just be in union with God all the time? We might think it comes from some outer authority, but it really comes from our own fears. If this is true, then ritual is used to overcome our fears, to bypass our own blocks to the experience of the sacredness at the core of the mundane.*

Waiting In Not Knowing

> ❀ *"Profound change and growth come when one is willing to let go and settle into the place of not knowing.*
> *To sustain this emptiness is to create enormous internal strength and wisdom,*
> *so we must take care not to rush in and fill it up."*
>
> Mentoring: The Tao of Giving and Receiving Wisdom,
> Chungliang Al Hung and Jerry Lynch

One day in March, I was strangely aware of being without commitments, deadlines or goals. Mid-afternoon, I went out with the dogs and we explored the newly exposed grassy areas. I sat on a birch log at the edge of our slowly melting pond. Nearby our dog Noon-sup played around the edges of the water while Girl was uphill digging for field mice in the snow. Suddenly, it occurred to me that I was simply waiting. Waiting in the unknown. I was ready for the next step but the next step was not clear, so I was sitting in the moment and trusting. It was an odd, serene feeling.

> ❀ *"Waiting in not knowing is not an easy thing to do in our culture. We often rush to fill the silence, to fill in the not knowing with doing. Something about not knowing bothers us. But it is a place of tremendous growth if we would but linger there a while.*

I have seen clients rush to fill the gaps. They get to a new place inside and immediately want to do something with it. The problem is that their thinking paradigm has not yet shifted, so they are just doing something different within the old model. We are wise to wait until there is more of a paradigm shift; until our model of understanding changes enough to support our new activity and we are not simply moving away from what not knowing feels like.

Back inside I checked my calendar. I was surprised to see that it was a week before Easter. It still seems odd for me not to be aware of the liturgical year and holy days of the church. And yet, though I was no longer planning my work and activities around the church year, it seems that on another level, I was honoring the sacredness of the season. Being in a state of simply waiting in the unknown is after all, a very appropriate place to be the week before Easter.

From Fear to Love: Call for a Paradigm Shift

Many today acknowledge the existence of human energy, but we don't fully understand it outside of our own fears and biases. Many New Age healers are themselves very concerned with 'catching and releasing' what they interpret as the negative energy of others. As such they work in a paradigm of fear and are not yet aware of the the full range and power of the paradigm of love.

If we are going to be intentional about working on an energy level, we need to be intentional about the paradigm within which we work. Otherwise we just end up with a new technique in an old framework. I believe that we are now ready to move into the paradigm of love, compassion and non-judgment. In other words, we are ready to move out of fear and into love/acceptance—the only internal place where healing really happens.

The paradigm within which we work is also the one which dominates our living. We cannot profess one for our healing practice or our spirituality, and live another in everyday life.

If we are in the paradigm of fear, it will show up in our work with clients no matter how much we profess to love.

In the paradigm of fear, practitioners hold a deep-seated "fear" of catching someone else's dis-ease or negative feeling energy. We have developed ways to literally shake off what feels like caught energy. When our zones of comfort have been breached, much of our time is spent discerning what is mine and what is theirs. We have probably all gone through this phase of interpretation of our experience.

There is a different interpretation of this experience, with more potential for healing. If we look at the experience of "caught energy" from a paradigm of love, it has a lot to teach us. First, if there is such a thing as caught energy, perhaps we caught it because there was a place in us for it to be caught; a place for it to adhere.

From the paradigm of love, we can challenge the concept of caught energy and say that the experience of discomfort exists in us—not because we caught someone else's energy but because their energy triggered or mirrored a similar energy within ourselves, with which we had not been in touch.

Thanks to the client or patient, our own 'stuff' is now rising into our conscious awareness for cleansing. When it does, we take the time to notice it, accept it and be loving and compassionate to ourselves. We listen to it without judgment. The client thus becomes the agent of our own healing. However, this will not happen if we live in fear and have a need to be perfect or better than our clients or patients. As much as we are able to 'be' with ourselves in non-judgmental love, we are able to be with our clients.

> ↪ *When we are in fear around others, no matter how unconscious that fear, then we are not able to be fully present.*

Why is this so? Because our fear will keep us on the defensive, which will create an energy barrier between us. This energy barrier does not allow for what Carl Rogers calls 'the three necessary elements for healing—empathy to the client by the practitioner, valuing of the client, and perceived trustworthiness of the practitioner by the client.'

The energy of love is one of acceptance and is experienced as compassion, openness, trust and value. In this state, we do not have to be perfect. We can acknowledge and accept our fear and the fear of those around us. We accept their dis-ease and we accept our own. In acceptance we are non-attached to the outcome and therefore do not experience the burn-out effect so common in many healing professions.

> ↪ *In acceptance, we release so much into the present moment that we access transpersonal levels of consciousness and become aware of the 'more than' in our midst.*

Love/acceptance is cleansing because it allows energy to flow and unconscious emotional blocks to loosen and release. When we sit in love with another there is no need to know if something is positive or negative. It just is. It is energy that was manifested in a certain way and in the presence of love is transformed. When we are not intentional about our paradigm, on some level, the client feels this and knows.

One of the best ways I have found to move into the paradigm of love/acceptance is to practice Inner Listening and be in a state of love and acceptance with myself. We can test to see if we are in this state by asking ourselves:

- Is there anything in myself that I fear and avoid?
- Do I notice a lot of things I don't like in others?
- Am I able to be still and do nothing, or do I move away from silence?
- Do I feel loved even in the midst of my anger, fear, loneliness and grief?
- Do I allow myself to be with all my feelings, or do I judge some as unacceptable or bad?"

Honoring the Sacred in our Very Midst— Call for a New Reformation

The first reformation gave people permission to be closer to God. The Bible was printed in German and for the first time was in the hands of the average person. The reformation claimed that priests are no longer needed to mediate God to the people. Each person has direct access to God.

However, there are still barriers to God, all of them humanly conceived. Some of these barriers occur when we confuse doctrines and rituals with what they represent. They do not have power in and of themselves.

> *A ritual is but a tool for altering our senses, for creating enough disassociation so we may surrender our attachments long enough to become aware of the sacred in our very midst.*

It is time to release God from the bondage of our own thinking. The church can have a unique place in the new reformation. Rather than take a defensive stance and see the call for inner growth and a deeper personal spirituality as a threat, it has the opportunity to get back to its original purpose of being God's love in the world by offering itself as a place for self actualization and the experience of God.

Since our inner world is reflected in the outer, the church can be a place where we own our projections onto others, share what is happening inside, notice behavior with each other, check out our assumptions, have our conflicts and learn in a mutually supportive, loving environment.

If we are not willing to do the inner work necessary to accept and love ourselves, we will not be able to love and accept others. If we are not willing to examine what the outer world is reflecting about our inner world, and if we are not willing to reclaim those parts of ourselves which we have judged, projected and repressed, we will see evil in others and fear them as much as we unconsciously fear ourselves. The saving grace of the church is truly God's love as exemplified in Jesus. But we have moved away from his love by getting bound up in judgments, projections and heady doctrines for our own justification. We preach love while unconsciously continuing the cycle of rejection leading to repression and fear.

> *As victims of our own judgment and fearful of our feelings and pain, we victimize and fear others in the name of God. It doesn't have to be this way.*

Religious education can begin to include more classes on the human experience of God. Pastors and lay persons can be taught to use Inner Listening tools in order to learn to lovingly be with themselves rather than projecting their 'stuff' onto others. These tools not only benefit the pastor, they also affect the congregation as permission is given to let go of Christian stereotypes. It is time to be our true self, do inner work, discover and develop gifts, share our journeys and grow together, supported by God's love. Sermons can then become more relevant to daily life and along with the worship service, help us to deepen our spirituality, connect with love, ourselves and each other as we remember who we really are.

> *It is time for a new reformation. It is time to realize that there is nothing that need stand between us and the Mystery we call God.*

Concluding With Gratitude

This book is the story of my journey as I have perceived it. I have shared enough to tease my friends, "You will know the book has been published when you see me walking naked in town with a bag over my head." But much has also been left unsaid.

There have been many people and situations to which I owe tremendous thanks. So if you have had a part in my life's journey, no matter how small or seemingly insignificant, no matter if we knew pleasure or pain together, know that I send you love and much appreciation.

Whatever comes of this manuscript, it has already been a blessing. And as I birth this book and begin to share it, I have a profound sense of self acceptance and belonging. Perhaps I have had a place in this world all along, right where I was—somewhere between double trouble and infinity.

 Somewhere between double trouble and infinity lies the present moment.

Part Four

Random Reflections
on the Soul Path

Clinical Spirituality

Early one day I happened to catch a morning show segment on how doctors were integrating spirituality into their practice. The doctor was examining a patient, holding the stethoscope and asking, "How is your relationship with God?" I gasped, then laughed at the TV, "I'd rather tell you how my bowel movement is!"

The question seemed so out of context, so out of place. The doctor knew that spirituality is an important part of health, but did not have the experience or training needed on the subject. All he had was the question. What would he say if I, with no medical training, got hold of a stethoscope and offered to give someone a physical exam?

I do feel delighted that the medical establishment has begun to integrate spirituality into medicine. It should never have been taken out in the first place. However, the way in which it is reintegrated is an important issue. Doctors must understand that the long hours and intense training, practice and devotion necessary to make them a good doctor are not unlike the hours of work and dedication required to become a good spiritual director. Medical training alone does not make one capable in the field of the spirit, and vice versa.

My fear is that spirituality and mindful living will become a new tool wrapped up in the same old dysfunctional, disempowering paradigm, offering easy answers which miss the depths of the journey to fearless compassion, non-judgment, love and grace. So much of the self-actualization movement seems to be a means to "success" as the western world defines it, and the tools of the soul path are used for the profit of the ego.

On the Body

> *The body is a vehicle for experiencing the sacred.
> It is the only part of us that lives full time in the
> here and now.
> By tuning in to it, we can live in the present
> moment.*

"I hate my body. I've tried many diets all my life and never lost much or kept it off. I'm sure that life would be just fine if only I could lose some weight," said my client. She was fighting a serious overweight problem and eating disorder.

After a few sessions she began to practice Inner Listening with herself. She was beginning to accept that her body was her best friend, helping her be aware of what she was feeling.

> *Treating the body as an evil keeps us from being with it,
> from being in the present moment and, ultimately, from the
> Mystery we call God.*

A year later she began to rise around 4 am and go for walks. One morning I peeked in as I passed by her office. She had a deep serenity about her and seemed to quietly glow. "Boy, you look so radiant. What is happening with you?" I asked.

With a big smile, she said, "Rather than just eat, I'm now writing down my feelings whenever the urge to eat comes on. At first it was difficult, but after a while I noticed that it became easier to bypass the compulsive urge to eat and write instead."

Soon she did not need to write down her feelings as much as she had developed easy access to them. When she was hungry, she simply asked herself what she was feeling. If she was really hungry, she ate an appropriate low fat meal. If she was moving away from feelings, she did not eat but simply allowed herself to be with her feelings.

She lost almost ten pounds a week, until she was sixty pounds lighter. She still has a way to go and the weight loss will probably slow down as she approaches a more healthy weight range. It seems as though she will make it, because she is not on a diet as much as a whole new way of being with her body and her feelings. That new way has led her to explore her outer surroundings more as well. She has gone into restaurants, attended concerts, and made new friends—all things she had not felt comfortable doing before because of her self abhorrence. Now she is enjoying life.

At one time in human history it seems that the body was a hindrance to spirituality, an evil. Now, it is pretty much accepted that any true spirituality must be fully embodied. I like that because it means acceptance of the body and its earthy gifts.

> *Accepting the body is accepting what the God/Source has created. To judge it is to put ourselves above God/Source.*

Accepting goes with the flow of the Sufi phrase,

"....until everything belongs and is accepted."

One day, out of the blue, she asked for a session. She wasn't sure why. In fact, she realized that what she was feeling was a sacred presence and she wanted help to simply stay with it instead of moving away. About one hour into the session, she was experiencing this embodied sacredness.

Noticing that she was radiant with energy from head to toe, I asked her if she wanted to stay for a while and savor it. She did. I left and told her to close the door when she left.

> *Sometimes you just know when to get out of the way.*

On Education

I love education and I hope to always be a life long student. But I have noticed that like everything else, it can be a tool to avoid the present or a tool to move into the realization and actualization of the soul.

There is nothing wrong with education of itself, but if it is used as a tool to avoid some challenging work that needs to be done now, then think again. If it is used to replace growing in the realization of true self-worth with outside affirmation, then think again.

I once met a person who just loved a popular author on spirituality. She read all his books and met with friends to talk about his writing on self-realization and mindfulness. I was familiar with the author and knew that he wrote frequently about coming to his awareness through a regular meditation practice. "Oh," I said, "so you have a regular meditation practice?" "No," she offered and looked at me strangely, "I just like his books."

It is not uncommon to move away from ourselves by buying and reading book after book, if we focus on reading rather than living the knowledge. Instead of being empowered, we give our power away, missing the very message of the books.

> *Looking out there for the answer, we grasp and grasp and are never satisfied.*

On the Ego

I sense that the ego is the part of ourselves that makes sense of the world and causes us to feel individuality or uniqueness within the world. It is a common modern practice to belittle and blame the ego. Many spiritual leaders make an effort to destroy the ego or at least not live from it. I think this is a deceptive practice.

I believe we are never without ego; it just becomes more subtle and looks more 'spiritual' or acceptable in our circles. I cannot think of any new age gurus, or old age ones for that matter, who did not have a strong ego. Sometimes the ego which fools itself into thinking it does not exist is the most insidious and dangerous kind. Better to accept our egos and work with them in the transformational process than pretend we can work around them or get rid of them.

It is said that matter is not destroyed, it just transforms.

> ∞ *It is time to stop trying to suppress or destroy the ego, and instead transform it into a vehicle of awareness and organization which promotes humility, compassion, love, understanding, grace, and peace.*

The ego is not evil in and of itself. It has been given a bad name and blamed for our selfishness and shortsightedness. Without an ego we would not learn what it is we are here to learn or have the impulse to do and to be what it is we are here to do and to be. Our sense of separateness is as important as our sense of unity.

I think it is important not to be so quick to judge, blame and write off what is emerging from the darkness of our subconscious by simply saying "it's my ego," or worse yet, "it's your ego." Such labeling only hinders our ability to be with it and discover the ego's gifts.

> ∞ *Who is to say that what we so quickly label as ego isn't a sign of a movement of the soul as of yet unactualized?*

Saying that we can be ego-less and have no degree of self interest is a very dangerous kind of spiritual self-deception and is ironically egotistical. We may have transformed some of the aspects which make up components with in our ego's mechanism and as a result we may appear and indeed be coming from a more unitive (enlightened) perspective, but as long as we walk the earth, none of us are or will be without ego.

∞ *Let's work on aligning the personality*
with the soul.
Then the ego won't be such an issue.

On Judgments

Just as it is not possible to live without ego, it is not possible to live without making judgments. Every decision involves a judgment, an ability to weigh matters, and discernment among a variety of options. What we decide to eat, wear, buy or who we chose to spend our time with involves judgments. Those of us involved in mindfulness and the spiritual journey can get as hooked upon the evils of judgment as we do the evils of ego. But in order to live, in order to get up in the morning, we have to make judgment calls.

Perhaps we can distinguish between judging and discerning. A judgment labels the world in terms of good and bad (and rejects the 'bad' half), while discernment involves weighing the perceived evidence in order to make healthy choices.

When we try not to judge in mindfulness meditation, we simply notice our thoughts and reactions without placing value on them. They just are. We are then discerning that it is good to sit and notice without judging!

On Answers

Sometimes seekers get hooked into thinking that they have to find answers, and have them for everyone else as well. This is just another defense mechanism—a way of not being where we are. Answers make things more acceptable to our perception of the world and give us the illusion of a greater sense of control. Filtered through the eyes of an answer, we no longer experience the present moment.

> ☙ *By being caught up in finding answers to everything, we move away from the wonder and mystery of the present moment.*

In our society, the answer is more important than the process with which we came to the answer. In mindfulness and Inner Listening, the process by which we arrive at the answer is more important. The process offers clues about the source of the answer. Does it come from our soul or from our defensive needs? There will always be more questions to explore, and different perspectives to be with. The challenge is to discern a process of being with the questions which reveals the soul.

> ☙ *As the ego surrenders to the soul, we grow in compassion, love, simplicity, clarity and grace. Then we come to realize that answers are not as important as the integrity of the process with which we live the question.*

On Fear

> ☙ *Fear can be a sign that we are approaching*
> *the boundaries of our comfort zone.*
> *Dare we cross over into enemy territory and*
> *approach our shadow?*

One gift of the New Age movement is its greater recognition of the fact that we live so much in fear. Many of us have gotten in touch with our more obvious fears, but the subtle ones often remain unnoticed. However, just as in any religion, a rigid attachment to New Age thinking can cover our fears and justify our avoidance of deeper truth.

One of the ways I have seen this played out is in people's ways of handling everyday situations. When something is difficult, takes effort, concentration and determination, the convenient excuse is that "the universe must not want it to be". There is a difference between surrender and avoidance; between letting go and giving up. Responsibility brings challenges with it, inviting us to grow.

I have seen this in working with clients. And I have noticed it myself when I have an appointment at the dentist. If it is hard to make it to an appointment that we perceive as challenging and may be stretching our boundaries, we unintentionally set up road blocks (get lost, have other things to do, forget) which makes getting to the appointment difficult. Then we cancel it, saying that "the universe or God must not intend it to be."

Very possible. But what happened to the deeper need which initiated the appointment in the first place? Did we cling to our fear which took over under the guise of the universe? We might have great intentions but seldom implement or live out our potential. We run around in circles of avoidance, missing the true source of our power hidden in the depths of the soul. To free this power from the subtle traps which appear to be spiritual takes determination, trust and discernment. Lots of discernment.

When do we finally get past our fears to receive the help we need to grow? When the desire to grow is greater than our fear of growth. Or when the pain of being where we are now is greater than our fear of what may lie ahead.

However, fear is not always a roadblock, especially if we listen to it. A client was going through some challenging life changes. Among other things, she needed to find a place of her own to live. She came to a session with a desire to get rid of an inner voice of fear. The fear came to her thoughts in the voice of a child saying that she would never find the right place for her needs.

Obviously, like most of us, she didn't want to hear such negativity. But I was curious as to what exactly the voice was saying. As she spoke of it, she was listing her exact needs at the time. We then realized that rather than assume this voice of fear was bad, she would do well to listen to it and follow it, since it indicated the needs that wanted to be fulfilled. When she was with the voice, she realized that she had often neglected her needs. Now she would take responsibility for them. In this case, the voice of fear was that of her inner child, stating some real as of yet unmet needs.

> ✿ *We would be wise to learn to discern our fears rather than just write them all off as the opposite of love, and thereby judging them as unacceptable. Every thing has a purpose and even our fears can point to solutions.*

On Positive Thinking

Positive thinking is a good exercise if it is used to remind us to notice the beauty we do not see, or the glass half full. Positive thinking and visualizations are often successfully used to help cancer patients. Indeed many studies have shown the positive curative effects of visualization techniques.

We all know the effect of feeding negative emotions and ideas. We all have done it and we know that what we focus on grows. Positive thinking, though it may take a little practice, also grows into a more happy, positive and less judgmental outlook. Yet it also has its traps.

> 🌸 *Too often positive thinking is not unlike placing a fragrant potpourri over a locked trunk filled with rotting matter.*

It can be an avoidance technique with easy answers—a modern psycho-spiritual pill. The effort it takes to be positive in the midst of such darkness filled with hurt, angry and rotting stuff fools the practitioner into thinking that they are accomplishing something.

In Inner Listening practice, I do not encourage this technique. Rather, let's go directly to the darkness and I will be with you as you enter it, release the contents, examine them if need be, air out the trunk, and experience the sweet fragrance of love, acceptance, compassion, peace and joy flowing into it. If positive thinking is not working for you, it may be time to be with and accept what you are holding onto. Upon acceptance, the darkness you held inside can be noticed, your true need can be honored and the symptoms of the previously unmet need released.

On Death

Death is a part of the "life flow cycle" because, as we now know, the kind of healing that has eternal value can take place on many different levels. The avoidance of death is no longer an adequate definition for healing. Indeed, when we stop fighting death and focus on living love instead, death may be but a beautiful compliment to a life well lived. Death is the final connection, as we know it, to wholeness.

It is important that we get in touch with our own death. Image it, be with it. That old saying remains true: If we are afraid of dying, we are afraid to live.

> ❀ *Those who live in the fear of death, do not really live. But those who live surrendered to the fact that any moment may be their last, will love every moment, live life to its fullest and have no regrets.*

On Spiritual Direction and Inner Listening

The simplicity of spiritual direction and Inner Listening can be deceptive. There are no bells and whistles. No one to tell us about ourselves, reveal secret knowledge or give us the image of our spiritual guides. There is no therapist to put a label on us which offers us the answer to "what's wrong with me?" Because for the spiritual director and Inner Listening mentor, *nothing is wrong!*

> ❀ *All is complete and whole in the moment, and when you let go of the need for answers and for bells and whistles, you come to a place of compassion and love and discover the wholeness that was always there.*

On Those Who Walk Their Soul Path

> ∞ *Profoundly simple and grace filled—*
> *such is the soul path.*

And these are words that describe those who walk it.

Very much in the moment, they observe and allow what is. Being centered and at peace with themselves, they have no need to change or convince others of the "rightness" of their way in order to feel good about themselves. They have an inner focus which is sharp, clear and golden. Little clutters or distracts their intention to live by the inspiration of God within. They are not afraid to grow or to seek help in growing. They overflow with love and appreciation. They live in, but not of the world.

Do not be surprised if they approach you as they would a friend, because they are already living a deeply connected life. And in their presence, for just a moment, you touch your own unique and golden Truth. You feel affirmed, accepted, whole and loving. Then you pass it on.

On Religious Institutions and the Perception of Good and Evil

> ∞ *Sacredness involves mystery.*
> *When we start naming the mystery, we begin to*
> *remove ourselves from it.*

Labeling and categorizing is the first step to "controlling" the Mystery called God which we just knew as children but now fear as adults. Then we spend the rest of our lives trying to let go of our compulsion to control. Ultimately, we must face our fears.

God 'is'. No categories apply. When Moses asked the voice from the bush, "Whom shall I say has sent me?" he received the answer, "Tell them, 'I AM has sent me.'" That says is all.

At some point on the journey, the doctrine and rigidity of the institutional path is no longer so much a means for self discipline, challenge and confirmation of the common faith, as it is a hindrance to self actualization. Eventually, we hunger for the experience of the sacred in our everyday life.

> To enter into the presence of the sacred, we have to let
> go of all the 'shoulds', and experience
> the moment—the Mystery—
> unfolding in peculiar and synchronistic ways.

To see the face of Christ in everyone, as the Benedictines practice, we have to let go of our labels, judgments and opinions, many of which are upheld, formally or informally, by the religious institution and its members.

In many ways it seems as if the institution sanctions certain projections. Not unlike the Jewish laws of Biblical times allowing the stoning of the woman caught in adultery, the laws or doctrines of our religious institutions encourage us to see 'good and evil' out there instead of looking inside ourselves.

> What if everything at the present moment
> is God?

Is it not true that those who go through life crying, "Get thee behind me, Satan," are simply seeing their own inner fears manifesting as some outwardly dark spiritual force. This manifestation is what keeps us, especially 'religious' or 'spiritual' people, from self-actualization and individuation. By holding onto the concept of darkness 'out there', we never get past it to see the truth "in here".

And what if these dark and condemning emotions, these thoughts and judgments do manifest as an energy "out there"? Then the irony is that we are creating the very thing we fear, and with each judgment and fear we feed this external 'evil.' Is it not again ironic that our actions to rid ourselves of it actually cause it to grow?

Only true and pure love can transform the energy of our fears into fuel for growth and healthy living. Only love can pierce the darkness and help us to face our fears.

> ෴ *Fear does not remove fear. Only love casts out fear.*

I've seen this again and again in Inner Listening sessions. By being compassionately present to the trapped emotions of fear inside ourselves, we allow ourselves to feel them and release them. Then we no longer need to project them out onto the world.

> ෴ *For many, the first step in the transformation process*
> *from fear to love is prayer.*
> *Prayer is our response to the movements of our*
> *soul stirring underneath the cluttered darkness*

As I reflect back, I see how my church experience helped me grow in compassion, spiritual understanding and public speaking ability. I feel tremendous gratitude for the time I ministered in the church and deeply appreciate opportunities I have today to bring the tools of Inner Listening to clergy and lay people.

More and more, it seems that people are seeking the experience of the soul and desiring to align their lives with their inner truth.

Pastors sometimes like telling people what and how to "think theologically". For some in the congregation this disempowers their own ability to produce meaningful theology from their spiritual life experiences.

In a time when we humans seem bent upon pushing and proving our own rightness of opinions onto others, we need more teachers and preachers who can help us access the inner reservoirs of love and wisdom which lay untapped in the depths of our own souls.

The passage from Jeremiah expresses this prophetically:

But this is the covenant that I will make with the house of Israel after those days, says the Lord:

"I will put my law within them, and I will write it on their hearts; and I will be their God, and they shall be my people. No longer shall they teach one another, or say to each other, "Know the Lord," for they shall all know me, from the least of them to the greatest..."

Jeremiah 31:33-34

On Emotions

When we journey on our soul path we do not cling to and feed upon our emotions. Rather, we observe them, feel them, and recognize them for what they are, while remaining centered in the present moment.

> *The present moment is always love.*
> *When we move outside of love we know that we*
> *have moved outside the present moment.*

Our emotional energy is emitted into our body and its surroundings. As a result, we might feel a hormonal haze, depressed fog, or angry static. Perhaps it is not unlike what in the old days was termed possession, except that it is not so much what possesses us as what we ourselves possess and to which we cling and feed.

For me, the prayer, "deliver us from temptation", set into modern terms, might say, "keep us from grasping; keep us from clinging on to that which gets us out of touch with our divine nature."

> *There is no emotion we need fear. If we are not able to*
> *experience love in the present moment it is usually a sign*
> *that an emotion we fear is trapped inside of us.*
> *Once this is experienced, really felt, it is released*
> *and the love residing within us can emerge.*

Any emotion that is not felt will be projected onto others. So it is easy to discover what we are not allowing ourselves to feel by asking, "What am I reacting strongly to in others?", then asking, "Could it be that I have those feelings in me to but have denied them?"

On the Void

Just how much our judgments and fears keep us from experiencing the gifts of the soul is clear in these two contrasting experiences of the void.

The first example is of a man in an Inner Listening session, who comes upon a dark void. This person had a fear of the void because, for him, it meant that deep inside himself, there was nothing. Instantly, he sprang back into his intellect—the familiar arena of fear and judgments which he seemed to believe was his true identity. The place where fear was absent meant, to him, that he was absent.

For those of us who meditate, the void or dark place of nothingness is a welcome experience when we sit, surrendered in the presence of the Mystery we call God.

> *The experience of the "void" is that space between the human and the divine, which is bridged by the love and grace of the Mystery we call God.*
> *It is the seat of the soul.*

Another example is of a woman who had spent many hours in meditation and had come to a retreat to deepen her relationship with the divine. Looking within was not new to her.

She shared, "When I am in meditation, I encounter a void. I'm not sure what to make of it."

I asked her to describe the void.

"I feel still, simple and peaceful, but so empty, it concerns me! I feel safer with my thoughts."

I suggested that this void was a gift and asked her what it would be like to stay with it and she said that she would like to try and went off to continue her meditation.

I did not receive any religious training regarding the void. In fact, it was never mentioned, but I had a sense that it is not held favorably. My supervisor was surprised when I shared with him that I had encouraged my client to stay with the void if she experiences it again. I'm not sure why he was surprised. If I had not had such a conflict about inner/outer authority, I might have asked him.

Indeed, the void came back to her and, sitting through it, she came to deepen into the sacredness of the experience. She was breaking new ground for her relationship with God.

Is it not fascinating, how our judgments color our ability to be with something? More and more I experience the truth in "until everything is accepted and belongs" and "God is love, God is experienced in the moment, and the moment is love, the moment is God, all that is, is God."

Of what are we afraid?

On False Love

Real love is never deceiving. But chances are, we have practiced deceiving under the guise of love. Have you ever been given or offered a criticism prefaced with "I say this out of love?" Have you ever made or been offered a luncheon date and the intention was not to enjoy lunch together but to nail into the person invited?

If a conversation is going to be difficult, let's be honest and say so, then decide together on the right place for the discussion. But when we project our stuff onto others in the form of accusations and blame, we are not capable of such honesty.

It is funny how we deceive ourselves and others with a false, demanding love that projects our fears onto others. We think we might be kind and soften the blow we are about to deliver, but more often than not it is to justify to our own ego what we know deep within our soul to be false in the first place.

> ❦Love begins in our own hearts. When we experience our inner divine love and begin to love ourselves, we can meet our needs honestly, openly and as adults.
> When we need others to love us in order to feel good about ourselves, we put the meeting of our needs onto them and may even manipulate them into meeting those needs, we have not taken responsibility for ourselves.

In some ways, it seems to me that a passionate love for another can be false as well. For it is not the other that we love but what we need in the other that we do not see in ourselves. This love has strings attached and soon dies when the flames of passion burn out.

Someone whose marriage broke up after 12 years once shared with me that she had finally started to experience real love. Until that time, she had loved and given with strings attached, in hopes of getting something in return. Then she would be inevitably disappointed and angry when her needs were not met.

On Present Moment Awareness

> ✦ I prefer to trust the moment.

Sometimes there are doctrines about the spiritual path which can serve as avoidance mechanisms. Sometimes we are told what to look for, and in looking for something not there, we don't see what is there.

A client's main desire was to heal past wounds and grow in love. He was told by others to look inside for an inner child to 'talk to', but all he was experiencing was a small, helpless fetus. It was frustrating and disappointing not to find find an inner child to converse with.

"Why not be with the fetus, then?" I asked him.

"What good is being with a helpless fetus? I can't talk to it. This is ridiculous." he retorted.

"Why not trust what your body is giving you? Your reaction against the idea of being with the fetus seems to be very strong," another friend suggested. "Is there something you might be avoiding here?"

The client then agreed to be with the experience. After sitting through his strong adverse reaction and imaging the fetus in his hands, tears welled up in his eyes and he whispered in surprise, "This is what I need to do."

How perfect the fetus was for helping him grow in love. With the little child, he could have escaped into heady conversations, but there was no such escape with the silent presence of an unborn being. All he could do was sit and love, for this fetus was love itself. There was no question that he had found what he was seeking when he finally received what he had been given.

> ✦ *Seldom do we seek something which is not already given to us. All we need to do is let go of what we are grasping in order to receive what we seek.*

On Labels

Our society relies heavily upon labels. We are quick to classify a person as alcoholic, schizophrenic, manic depressive, etc. Sometimes those who seemed to have the most difficulty entering into wholeness are those who have attached themselves to labels and incorporated those labels into their identity. Oddly enough, they seldom exhibit signs of the label in sessions of spiritual direction or Inner Listening because every effort is made to help them stay in the moment.

Labels, it seems to me, are not in the moment. Instead, they describe the symptoms we exhibit when we move away from the present moment. A label can become a way to avoid responsibility for our emotional response to daily events.

> �֎   *Classifying and categorizing things,*
> *people or feelings has the effect of keeping us from*
> *deepening into our inner experience.*

Indeed we become fearful that the symptoms the label describes will return, should we stay with what we are feeling.

When Donna, a client who was once institutionalized for depression after a grievous experience, came to direction, she told me, "I am a manic depressive. I feel sad a lot and take medication for it. But I often take extra doses because when I'm feeling down I have lots of anxiety about getting depressed again and being institutionalized."

What a self-perpetuating, vicious circle. I began by reassuring her that occasional sadness is to be expected. Being aware of sadness and facing it is important.

"But how can you tell me that feeling down is o.k.?" She sincerely thought that feeling sad meant something was wrong with her.

I encouraged her to just be with the anxiety and sadness instead of trying to run from it. "Let's ask what the sadness might be telling you. What are your needs right now?"

She discovered that when she was feeling down, she wanted the company of others. Little by little she was coming to experience that her sadness simply pointed to some needs, and she could then meet these needs.

After a year of monthly Inner Listening sessions, things slowly began to change. One day she called to say that she had been feeling sad. But instead of becoming anxious and taking extra medication, she sat and breathed with the sadness. Pretty soon, she entered a very calm and serene space within herself. But just as it took years to learn to avoid a feeling, it can take years to learn to stay with one, especially if one has a label, sanctioned by professionals, that justifies avoidance.

Spiritual direction and Inner Listening cut through the symptoms upon which we stick labels and gets to the heart of the wound, enabling us to become mindful of our deeper unmet needs. Once we touch these needs with compassion and non-judgment, we can begin to responsibly address them.

On Identifying With Our Fears

It is not unusual for clients in a direction session to find that they are facing fears that were bottled up from many years of wounding and neglect. One client watched his fears open a door and simply march past him during inner visualization. Then he started patting himself on the arms and chest. I asked what he was doing. He explained that he had identified so much with his fear that, since it left, he was wondering if he was still there!

This man had come to spiritual direction with the label of having multiple personalities. But once he learned to be in the moment and not avoid his feelings, he could sit with his fears, heal from painful past experiences, and get on with his life.

Present moment awareness or mindfulness helps us to observe our fears without identifying with them. We are more than our fears. Fears are but a conditioned response we hold on to and can also let go of. In a way, fear is a subtle tool for the avoidance of pain, because underneath fear lies an unattended wound filled with pain. Once we attend to the wound and feel the pain, the fear is released.

> ∽◇◯◌∕ *Fear does not grasp us —we grasp it.*

On Surrender

Most of our struggles come because we have not surrendered into the moment. Our fears and mistrusts all begin within ourselves and manifest on the outside as fear and mistrust of others.

> ✿ *If we could just be in the moment, we would*
> *know that love is all there is.*
> *Everything else we perceive is a misguided*
> *attempt, no matter how justified it seems, to ful-*
> *fill the need for love.*

When I was just beginning my direction practice, I had the honor of working with a few seminary students. They taught me so much and were such a gift. With one person in particular, I remember working on the issue of surrender. He had an important meeting with a committee which could make decisions that affect his life in important ways. At first, in talking about the committee he voiced fear of the power they had over him.

I challenged him: "Let's start by being with the members of the committee—not in fear, but in love. To do this, it is important to stay within your center of strength; your source of love within the core of your being. Meet them from that deep level of your soul. They will notice that strength and love which is the real you. The way they chose to be with that is up to them. In other words, turn it all over to God."

He came back from the meeting and reported feeling centered in a meeting which would normally throw him (or anyone else for that matter) off center. He reported how he felt love for those gathered, how they listened to his story and his honest responses to their questions.The meeting went very well, better than he could have planned. As I recall, he said something about God being very present and having a visible influence on everyone.

I once sold some pottery to a lovely woman who turned out to be married to the same man for thirty years. I asked her what enabled them to stay together through the trials of life. She said, "Love softens the way."

 Like sandpaper smoothes to the hard edges of wood, love softens our defenses.

On Love

As a pastor I have had the privilege of being with people in very personal and deep ways. They taught me much about life and death, and love.

So many wise and wonderful people. So much wisdom and love to share. How can we not stand in awe of the daily revelations of the divine?

I recall sitting on the floor by the chair of an elderly woman. She had a soft, angelic glow about her which contrasted with what I perceived to be once hard edges of pride and opinion. In the glow, I sensed that these edges were wearing down as she prepared for her transition into the world of spirit. I came to love this wonderful lady, so I decided to follow my impulse to tell her so.

"I love you." It felt natural and right to say.

She turned to me, "You know, in my family, no one ever said 'I love you'. It was implied, of course, but somehow not o.k. to say out loud."

"How do you feel about that? Would you like to have said it or heard it more?" I asked.

"Oh yes, I have a longing to say it to my children. Yet so much time has passed without saying it. How does one say 'I love you'?"

I suggested that when the feeling of love wells up inside of her, she be brave and just say it. It might be a gift that her children could carry with them long after she is gone.

We say 'I love you' for many reasons, but for me the best love has no strings, no expectations attached. I say it when I am touched by the manifestations of the inner spirit. When our conversation goes beyond opinions and judgments and touches upon our struggles to live and our experience of pain and compassion. When, by grace, we move one another into the moment, to love.

 To say 'I love you' is but an affirmation of what we know we already are.

RESOURCES FOR THE SOUL PATH

Bio-Spirituality: Focusing as a Way to Grow. Campbell, Peter A. Ph.D. and McMahon, Edwin M. Ph. D. (Chicago, Loyola University Press, 1985)

Liquid Light of Sex. Clow, Barbara Hand. (Santa Fe, Bear & Co, 1991)

Focusing. Gendlin, Eugene T., Ph.D. (Bantam Books, A Bantam New Age Book, 1981)

Seeking the Heart of Wisdom: The Path of Insight Meditation. Goldstein, Joseph and Kornfield, Jack. (Boston, Shambahala, 1987)

Psychological Astrology: A Synthesis of Junian Psychology and Astrology. Hamaker-Zondag, Karen. (New York Beach, Main: Samuel Weiser, Inc., 1990)

Wherever You Go, There You Are. Kabatt-Zinn, Jon. (New York, Hyperion, 1994)

A Path with Heart: A Guide Through the Perils and Promises of Spiritual Life. Kornfield, Jack. (New York, Bantam Books, 1993)

The Art of the Possible: A Compassionate Approach to Understanding the Way People Think, Learn and Communicate. Markova, Dwana, Ph.D. (Conari Press, 1991)

King, Warrior, Magician, Lover: Rediscovering the Archetypes of the Masculine. Moore, Robert and Gillette, Douglas. (New York, Harper Collins, 1990)

Medicine Cards: The discovery of Power through the Ways of Animals. Sams, Jamie and Carson, David. (Santa Fe, Bear & Co., 1988)

Living the Mindful Life: A Handbook for Living in the Present Moment. Tart, Charles. (Boston, Shambhala, 1994)

202

*The Joy of Feeling: Bodymind Acupressure, Jin Shin Do.*Teeguarden, Iona Marsaa. (New York, Japan Publications, 1987)

The Call and the Echo: Sufi Dreamwork and the Psychology of the Beloved. Vaughn-Lee, Llewellyn. (Brattleboro, Threshold Books, 1992.)

No Boundary: Eastern and Western Approaches to Personal Growth. Wilber, Ken. (Boston, Shambhala, 1979)

Star Guidance: Astrological Guidance for Life and Life Purpose. Lake, Gina, M.A.